MIND 2.0

How To Become Awesomer?

ANURAG RAI

Founder of Superhuman In You

www.superhumaninyou.com

MIND 2.0

Copyright © 2023 Superhuman Education Limited

All Rights Reserved. No part of this book may be reproduced or utilised in any form or by any means, digital, audio, or printed, without the author's written consent.

The author of this book does not dispense medical advice or prescribe the use of any technique as a form of treatment for physical or medical problems. Please consult with a physician or doctor if you have a medical condition. The information provided is solely on extensive experience and research. The actual results may vary from person to person.

SUPERHUMAN IN YOU
www.superhumaninyou.com

Contents

Start with a Stop 7

Who is this Guy? 8

Thank You Note 9

An Invitation Before We Begin 10

CHAPTER 1 14
How Well Do You Know Your Brain?

CHAPTER 2 18
Slowing Down

CHAPTER 5 25
The Three Principles of Psychology

CHAPTER 6 27
Our thoughts create our reality. Or do they?

CHAPTER 7 34
Mind: A Beautiful Servant or A Dangerous Master

CHAPTER 8 40
Human Consciousness

CHAPTER 9 45
9 Laws of the Human Mind

CHAPTER 10 48
7 Daily Practices to become the CEO of your brain

CHAPTER 11 63
Problem Vs Situation - *Not every Problem is a Problem*

CHAPTER 12 67
Neuroplasticity - *The Brain That Continuously Changes Itself*

CHAPTER 13 70
Re-inventing You

CHAPTER 14 75
Understanding Emotions

CHAPTER 15 79
Present Moment is the only reality

CHAPTER 16 82
The Secret behind "The Secret"

CHAPTER 17 88
How to get Things Done? The Anti-Procrastination Formula

CHAPTER 18 92
~~Managing~~ Ending Stress

CHAPTER 19 98
Surrender Like a Warrior

CHAPTER 20 102
Feeling the Fear is Not Bad, But Living in Fear is

CHAPTER 21 109
It's Not About Time Management

CHAPTER 22 118
Positive Possibility Thinking

CHAPTER 23 123
The Power of Receiving

CHAPTER 24 128
How to become Unfuckwithable?

CHAPTER 25 131
Leading with EQ - *How to Positively Influence Others?*

CHAPTER 26 138
How to Make or Break Habits on Demand?

CHAPTER 27 143
Why Have a Morning & a Bed-Time Ritual?

CHAPTER 28 149
Meditation & Mindfulness

Resources to Help 158

Start with a Stop

Where are you? Are you here? Do you feel the weight of this book in your hands? Do you feel your breath? Do you feel your fingers? Do you feel your toes? Take a deep breath in. Feel your lungs expanding, and breathe out letting all your thoughts and tensions go with a big sigh ..... aaaaaah

Do this exercise every time you pick this book to continue reading. You will gain more from your awareness than from the information between the pages.

Your Biggest Fan

Anurag

Who is this Guy?

Let's start by answering the first question first, especially for those of you who don't know me. I am just an ordinary guy who gets to show extraordinary people like yourself, how extraordinary they really are. If you ever get to speak to my wife, she will tell you all about how ordinary I am.

I am not a Phd in Literature. In fact, I did not even study literature in school. English is also not my first language. So, I apologise in advance for my simple language and grammatical errors. I intentionally refused to get this book edited, because I want you to meet me as I am. If you were attending one of my workshops or seminars, you would not have an editor editing my words, then why here. This book is not about me, it's about you.

But I know some of you may be interested in my credentials, so here they are. I am an MSc in Psychology, a Certified Master NLP Practitioner, Best Selling Author of the book The Power Within, and an Award-Winning Coach. My work has been featured in major publications such as Fox News, USA Today and MarketWatch. My clients include Sports personalities, celebrities, police officers, and powerful leaders from all walks of life.

Here's what some of my clients say about me:

> *"Anurag brings out the genius within you."*
>
> – **Graham** *CEO of a Technology Firm*

"Coaching I received has transformed my life and business"

– **Martin** *Business Owner – Pubs & Property*

"I can only describe Anurag as someone with magical capabilities at unlocking your potential"

– **James** *Business Owner – Brand & Design*

While I am grateful for all the above, I also know that none of these matters. What matters is what I can do for you. You, the person reading this. My goal with this book is to create a space for you to meet the most **extraordinary** you.

Your Biggest Cheerleader

Anurag

Thank You Note

I want to thank you. Not just for the money you invested, but also for your trust, commitment, and time you will be investing. I appreciate it, and I don't take it lightly. My goal is to serve you as powerfully as possible in this book. And hopefully make this a thought-provoking, insightful and transformational read. Let's get started.

Loving you

Anurag

An Invitation Before We Begin

Just before we begin, I have an invitation for you. We live in an information age, so much so that most of us consider ourselves experts, with the world of resources at our fingertips. So, every time we hear a new piece of information, we listen to it to agree or disagree. The problem with that approach is that we never really get a new insight. Because we think we already know. No insight can ever occur from a place of knowing.

My Coaching is based on insights. In other words, it's not about what I say but what you hear. So, my invitation for you is to read as if you are reading fiction. Let the words flow within and around you. There may be things that make sense and then there will be things that don't but don't spend too much time analysing things. Spend more time reflecting on your own thoughts, rather than what you read. Read with an open mind and your life will never be the same again. I have seen this happen over and over again with my clients.

This book will change your life if you allow it to.

Your Coach

Anurag

Please Read All the Chapters in Sequence...

CHAPTER 1
How Well Do You Know Your Brain?

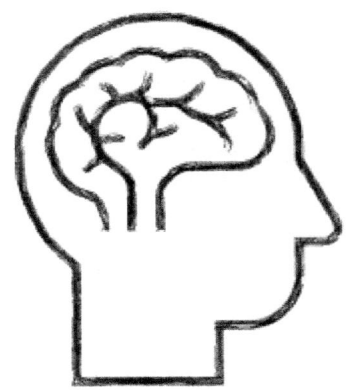

Our brain is one of the most powerful tools we will ever own, but a lot of us never take the time to understand it. Let's test your knowledge about your brain.

How many bits of information do you think the brain receives per second?

Answer: 11 million

Out of those 11 million bits, how many do you think the conscious mind can process?

Answer: 40

CHAPTER 1

Now imagine a picture made up of 11 million dots. Then take away all the dots and leave just 40. Would you ever know what the true picture was? No. But this is what is happening every second in our experience. Our brain deletes, distorts, and generalises information to create its own reality. Usually, the 40 dots it chooses are based on past choices and beliefs.

Now look at image 1 below:

Image 1

Do you see a young or an old lady in the picture? Based on my experience, around half of you will see a young lady, and the other half will see an old woman. And if you have seen this before, you may see both.

Now let's look at image 2 below:

CHAPTER 1

Image 2

Again, based on my experience, half of you would see the dress colours as white and gold, and another half will see it as black and blue. *(If you are reading this book in paperback copy, then the above image would be black and white. So, to do this exercise you will have to search the image of this dress on internet. Just google – "The dress illusion" and you will find the image.)* But it's not just what we see. Let's look at how we process the information we hear.

CHAPTER 1

Go to https://superhumaninyou.com/htba and watch the video titled **Yanny/Laurel**. What did you hear? Based on research half of you would hear the sound as 'Yanny', and another half would hear it as 'Laurel'.

So, the question we now face that which one of you is seeing or hearing it correctly. And the answer is NO ONE. We all are just using around 40 bits of information to create the full reality. You put two people in the same room, and they come out having different experiences. Imagine what this means for the way we communicate, the misunderstandings in our personal and professional relationships, and our understanding of our problems, situation and life in general. Over the next few pages, we will go over this topic in much detail. We will understand how our experience of life is more a reflection of our thinking than our reality. And how we can use this information to move forward and achieve our most 'impossible' goals.

CHAPTER 2
Slowing Down

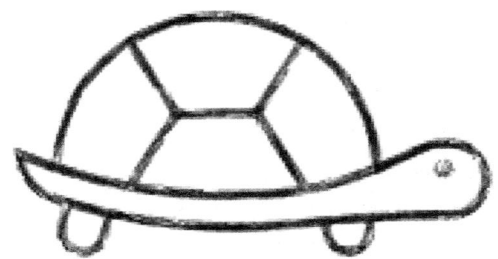

I am a big believer in slowing down to move fast. Most people are driving their cars with muddy windscreens, and when you ask them to stop and clean their windscreens, they say they don't have time. Useless **busyness** is damaging your **business**. And by slowing down, we don't mean working less. The reason why most people feel tired, burnt out or overwhelmed is not that they are doing too much; it's because they are thinking too much. You could be working 18 hours a day and still be very productive, very happy and very focused if your thinking is slowed down. So, by slowing down, we are referring to the pace and quality of your thoughts, not the movement of your hands.

Here's a story of a guy who saved a village by slowing down. Let's call him Mark. Mark was once sitting next to a river. Suddenly he noticed someone drowning at a distance.

CHAPTER 2

Straightaway he jumped in to save that person. But then he noticed more people drowning. He tried to save as many as he could. Soon other people from his village noticed this and started helping our guy. Three days went by, and no matter how hard they tried, they could never save everyone.

One day Mark just disappeared. Villagers thought he must have just given up, so they continued to save as many people as possible. On the third day (still no sign of Mark), there was no one else drowning anymore. Later that day, Mark appeared too. Villagers told him what had happened and that no one else was drowning anymore. To which Mark replied, "I know. It's because **I fixed the problem upstream.** It occurred to me that if people are drowning here, they must be falling somewhere. I went upstream and built gates and signs up to avoid people falling in the first place."

Slowing down Exercise: Think of a problem in your life/business. Then ask yourself these three questions:

1. **What's causing that?**

   ....

   ....

2. **And what's causing that** (your answer to question 1)?

   ....

   ....

3. **And what's causing that** (your answer to question 2)?

   ....

   ....

CHAPTER 3
Life Quality

Let's explore the most important question - **What does the quality of our lives depend on?** Does it depend on 'the physicality of life' or 'the experience of life'? Now, most people would say that it depends on the experience of life. However, they could argue that the experience of life depends on the physicality of life. But what if that's not true?

All our experiences are inner experiences. They happen inside us. It may seem like they are happening outside us, but in truth, we don't experience reality, we experience our interpretation of reality, which is an inner phenomenon.

For example, you may think that you are seeing these texts in front of you, but in reality, you are seeing these texts inside you. Light falls on the book, creates a reflection, goes into your

CHAPTER 3

eyes, creates an inverted projection, and sends this signal to your brain and you are seeing these texts inside you.

So, if all our experiences are inner experiences, and the quality of our life depends on our experiences, shouldn't understanding how our inside works, in other words, how our mind works, be the most important thing for human existence? Yet most people live their whole life without ever putting any effort into understanding the Mind. They try to solve the problems without ever understanding the <u>single source</u> that is creating them. They try to manage the symptoms, without taking a step back and dealing with the problem upstream – MIND MANAGEMENT.

So, they spend their entire life in survival mode. This book is about coming out of the survival loop and stepping into creation mode.

<u>Reflection Exercise:</u> Take a moment to reflect on your life/business problems. Are they problems or symptoms?

....
....
....
....
....
....
....
....
....

CHAPTER 3

CHAPTER 4

What will you learn?

This book is not about how to fix problems. It's about how problems are created. This book is not about stress or fear management. It's about where stress and fear come from. This book is not about reading it's about seeing. This book is not about information, it's about insights. And one powerful insight, followed by a decision, followed by an action, can change your life forever.

In the first part of this book, we will start by gaining a deeper understanding of how our mind works. We will explore how our thoughts, mind and consciousness together create our reality and experiences. Then in the second part, we will look at some powerful tools you can use to deal with emotional and

CHAPTER 4

mental health challenges. We will also look at ways you can improve your performance and so your results.

The book has a fresh approach when compared to most self-help literature. So be open to seeing your problems, life and the world from a new lens. The book will not teach you the 'right things' to do. Instead, it will help you see what's been ineffective in your life and what would be effective. It will help you redefine success and create a roadmap for how to achieve it.

CHAPTER 5
The Three Principles of Psychology

The three principles of psychology also referred to as the three principles, or the health realization, were introduced by Sydney Banks. Sydney Banks aka Syd Banks was a Scottish welder who after having an enlightening experience became a world-known philosopher, author, and lecturer.

The three principles suggest that we all create our own experience of reality using our thoughts, mind, and consciousness (the three principles). Figure below shows an analogy that we can use to understand this phenomenon.

CHAPTER 5

Think of our thoughts as DVDs, our mind as a projector, that projects our thoughts onto our consciousness (the screen). You project a scary thought, and you feel fear. You project a sad thought, and you feel sadness. You project a grateful thought, and you feel gratitude. **Any feeling results from your awareness of your thinking in that moment.**

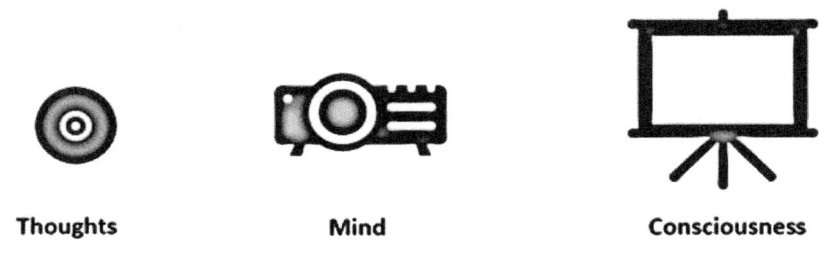

Thoughts　　　　　**Mind**　　　　　**Consciousness**

How we create our experience of the reality

CHAPTER 6
Our thoughts create our reality. Or do they?

"The fool only knows what he thinks; the wise man knows he's the thinker."

~ Syd Banks

You may have heard the saying 'our thoughts create our reality'. But how true this is? This phrase is often quoted in the law of attraction space (more on the law of attraction later). From my perspective thoughts alone do not create our reality.

CHAPTER 6

In fact, if we can learn to understand that our thoughts are not real, then they may have little to no effect on reality. However, our thoughts do create our experience of reality. This is the reason why two people who have been under similar circumstances may have different experiences of those circumstances.

There are events and then there are thoughts about those events. Our experience of an event is based on our thinking, and not on the actual event. Let me explain this by using an example. Let's say you are driving your car, and someone dangerously overtakes you. How would you respond to this? Most people would feel angry, frustrated, and annoyed. You may even horn and/or shout at them. Some of us may even choose to use our fingers as an added measure to express our feelings.

Now, what if you knew that the person overtaking you was rushing to the hospital where their loved one is counting their last breath? How would you feel then? Most of us will feel empathy and compassion for this person. The same thing happened in both scenarios and in both scenarios, you experienced the same level of inconvenience. But your feelings and experience have changed based on your thoughts about it. Now, you can either hire a private detective and find out why this guy overtook you, or you can choose to think that maybe he is attending an emergency. Because no matter what you think, the guy who overtook you remains unaffected. Your thinking creates your experience, not his.

The way we think influences our experience of reality, which then influences our response, which then creates our reality. So, thoughts may have some role in creating our reality. Another way how our thoughts shape our reality is by shaping our beliefs. Our beliefs are formed by thinking about something repeatedly until our brain records it as a belief. There is an old saying that "seeing is believing" but in reality, we don't believe what we see, we see what we believe. In other words, we only see what we are looking for. Here's an experiment. Go to https://superhumaninyou.com/htba and watch the video that is titled – Awareness Test.

Don't continue reading until you have watched the video.

Have you watched the video? Are you sure? Ok great. You may then continue reading the next paragraph.

In the video, the reason why you missed the man wearing a bear costume is that you were looking for the white players, so even though this weird creature walked past you, you did not see it. In chapter 1 we discussed how our conscious mind can only process 40 bits of information. The 40 bits that the conscious mind picks are often the bits that support our beliefs. Because for our brain, whatever has kept us safe so far must also keep us safe going forward. Remember the brain is designed to help us survive and not thrive. So, our thoughts lead to our beliefs which then limit what we see and thus limit our view/experience of reality.

My Experience with My Thinking

A few years ago, I had a restaurant business. This was my first business, so I was still young and learning. But regardless just after 6 months of opening, our business was growing every day, and I was planning to buy my next restaurant. But then one afternoon, one of my chefs came to my home and said that he will have to travel back to his country as his mum's health was very poor. He asked me for help. So, I gave him all the money I had on me. I felt good that I was able to help him.

CHAPTER 6

The same day in the evening, two guys in suits came into the restaurant and asked for this guy. When I asked who they were, they said they are from CID (Crime Investigation Department). I realised that my chef must have done something terrible, and he is not coming back. I also figured that I will not get back the money he borrowed from me. I could not sleep that night. I remember thinking why did he do this to me?

The following morning when I went to deposit the last 2 days' takings in the bank, I found that this guy also stole my chequebook and managed to forge my signature to take out all the cash from the bank. I felt something heavy in my chest and lost my ability to think. But then I recollected myself and managed to make my way to the restaurant. I knew that the restaurant must keep running as I had bills and wages to pay. I somehow managed to work in the restaurant but could not sleep again that night. The same thoughts kept repeating in my mind, "why would anyone do this to anyone?". My brain was running 100 miles an hour.

The next things got worse. As we were preparing to open the restaurant in the afternoon. A lady from the local council came to inspect the place. She was friendly and nice. The restaurant was still fairly new, so we were due an inspection. After about two hours of checking everything, she told me that she has found an issue with the wiring of the place. And so, it is not safe to operate until that issue is resolved. She shut the place and said we must resolve the issue before opening. I could not understand what was happening in my life. How would I get this resolved? I had no money on me as I gave it to my chef, no money in the bank as he took it all, and now even no incoming.

And just when I thought things could not get worse. A couple of days later, someone must have noticed that the restaurant

CHAPTER 6

is shut for two days, so they broke in. Because I blocked my bank account till things get resolved, I kept all-cash sales in the restaurant. The person who broke in stole all the cash as well as some other valuables including my laptop. I was young and inexperienced and did not have the right covers in place to be able to claim for any of the losses. I was on a visa, so I had no help from the local council or the government. In other words, I was fu***d. Badly.

I had bills and wages to pay plus the cost of repairs to get the restaurant open and there was no source of income. Closing the restaurant was not an option. Not because I was determined, but because my visa was based on my restaurant business. And I was not prepared to go back after losing all this money. So, I started thinking about what bills can I avoid. My biggest expense at that time was around 1000 pounds per month in rent for my flat. So, I decided to move out of my flat and move into the storeroom of my restaurant. Now because of the wiring issue, the lady from the council cut the electricity supply. So, there was no light or heating.

I spent the next 4 nights doing the same thing. I would sit in a corner on the floor with bin bags full of my clothes around me. And I would think all day and night – Why me? Why did this happen to me? I was a big believer in Karma. I believed if you did good things, good things happen to you. And if you did bad things, bad things happen to you. So, what bad had I done to deserve this? The more I had that thought, the more sad, full of guilt, and depressed I got. The more I asked, 'Why me?', the worse I felt.

But then on the fourth night, while I was sitting there in the corner having my usual thoughts, a new thought popped up. This time the thought was 'Why not me?'. There are thousands of little kids dying in war zone countries. Surely, they haven't

CHAPTER 6

done any bad karma. So, when bad things can happen to them, then why not me? I thought maybe it was not about good karma or bad karma. Maybe things just happen, it's what we do about it that matters. This new thought shifted my being. I went from feeling stressed and depressed to feeling empowered and grateful (because it could have been worse).

That was the first time I experienced the power of thoughts. I managed to borrow more money from friends and family and got a night job for some time, to get things back to where they were. It took 12 months of hard work and possibility thinking (we would talk about this later) and the restaurant was in profit again.

Since becoming a coach, I have seen the power of thoughts over and over again. A client once told me that one of his employees really annoys him. I asked my client, "Are you annoyed just now?" and he replied, "Yes, very much". I then asked him, "Is your employee with you just now?". He replied, "No". I then said, "If he annoys you out and he is not with you just now, why are you annoyed now?". And I paused. And he realised that it was not his employee that is annoying him. It's his thoughts about the employee or what the employee does, that annoys him.

I want you to know that no matter where you are, what you are dealing with, and how bad it looks, you are just one thought away from feeling better and one thought away from feeling worse. Which thought would you choose? While you cannot choose your first thought, you can always choose your next or last thought.

I would like to share with you another story. You may have already come across some version of it. Once there was an old monk who was trying to teach one of his students, the power of thinking. The old monk said to the student, "Each one of us has two wolves constantly fighting in our heads. A wiser and more positive wolf and a foolish and more negative wolf". The student asked, "Master, which one of the two wins?". The old monk replied, "The one you feed more".

CHAPTER 7
Mind: A Beautiful Servant or A Dangerous Master

"Mind is not brain. Neither is it a thing or a thought. It is a psychic force that acts as a catalyst and turns thought, conscious or unconscious, into the reality you now see."

~ Syd Banks

Everything in and around our universe is governed by the mind. And when I talk about mind, I am referring to 3 levels of mind. Our mind, other's mind, and the mind of the

CHAPTER 7

universe. We cannot control other's mind or the universal mind. We can only control our mind. So, the less energy we waste trying to control these, the more energy we have to control ours. And while we cannot control others', or universal mind, we can still influence them. But to do so, we must first learn to control and manage our mind.

"To the mind that is still, the whole universe surrenders."

~ Lao Tzu

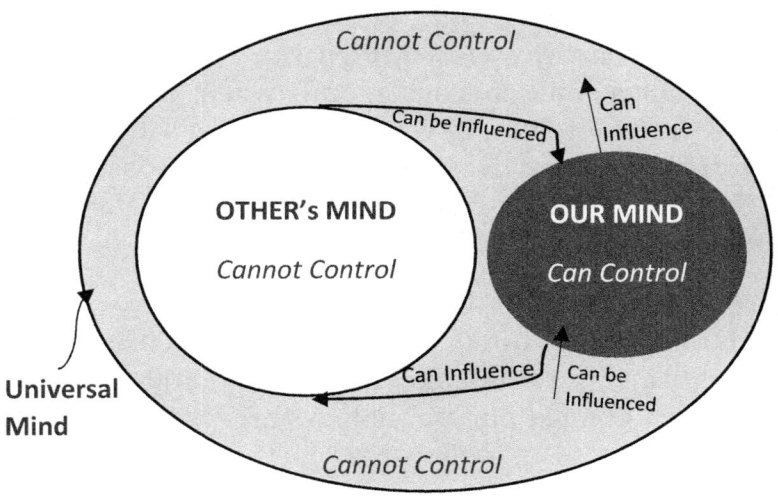

A complicated map of common sense

In this chapter, we will focus on understanding the mind in general. We will then look at ways to control and manage our mind. I will share 4 simple strategies that you can use to constantly stay motivated, committed, creative and in a higher emotional energy state. But first, let's understand the difference between the mind and the brain.

CHAPTER 7

The Lemon Experiment

Let's do an experiment. Read the instructions and then close your eyes to do it. Imagine that you are holding a big juicy lemon in your hand. I now want you to imagine that you are cutting this lemon in half. Then take half slice of the lemon and start squeezing it in your mouth. Notice what it tastes like and notice what it smells like. Once you have done this full visualisation open your eyes and read the next paragraph. Make sure you do this experiment before reading further.

So, if you are like most people and if you did the experiment properly with your eyes closed, then you would notice that there was saliva built in your mouth when you imagined squeezing the lemon juice in your mouth. That saliva is there to neutralize the acid in the lemon juice, but there is no lemon juice. Even though it's a simple experiment, there are some profound lessons.

1. We are not our Brains.
2. Our Brain does not understand the difference between reality and our thinking.
3. We can change our physiology just by changing our psychology.

Before we begin the discussion on understanding the human mind let's first agree on what the mind is not. Your mind is not your brain. The brain has thoughts, the mind processes them. The brain is physical, but the mind is not. Your brain is confined to your skull, but your mind can not be confined. I invite you to think of the mind as three different segments working together to create our response to situations at conscious, subconscious and emotional levels.

CHAPTER 7

The subconscious mind is the part of our brain that stores information and then creates responses without our initiative. As we go through life we learn behaviours, beliefs and 'normal' ways to respond to situations. All this information is stored in our subconscious and whenever there is a trigger, it creates a response without our conscious choice or initiative. The subconscious mind is very powerful, and research suggests that it is responsible for around 95% of our brain activity. It manages most of our body's functions, like eating, breathing, digesting and creating memories. We have no control over this mind, but we can over time interrupt past patterns and programming to create new patterns and programming. We cannot choose to not program the subconscious mind. It's programmable by design.

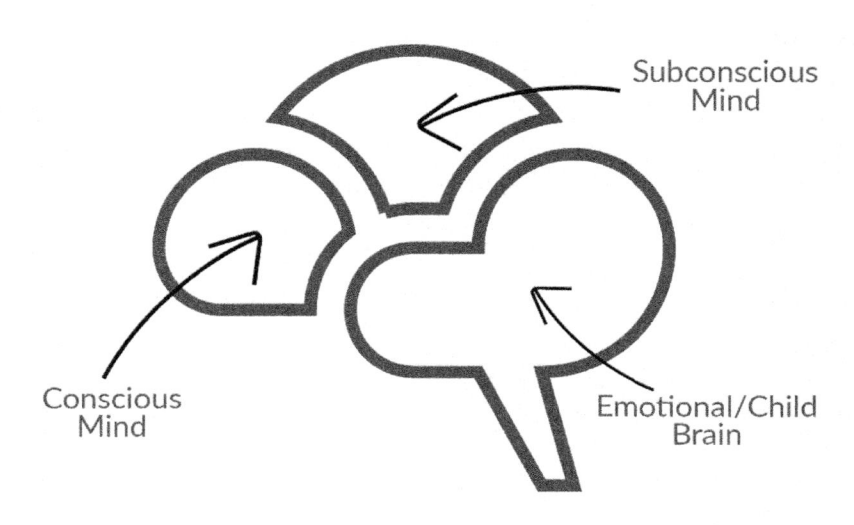

A simplified understanding of the human mind

CHAPTER 7

The emotional/child brain is like a child. It follows the laws of the jungle. Survival is the number one priority. It is important for the emotional or the child brain (also referred to as chimp brain) to be right as that would mean they are a valuable member of the community. It is also important what others think because if members of the community do not like you or see you as valuable, they may throw you out of the community. And it is hard to survive in the jungle on your own. Obviously today we don't live in jungles and so what others think has no impact on our survival. But because we cannot control this part of the brain, the first thought or response would always be an extremely emotional one, as if it is a threat to survival.

Finally, the third segment of our mind is what we refer to as our conscious mind. All activities in the prefrontal cortex of the brain are related to our conscious mind. We can also understand this as the logical mind. This is the segment of our mind that we control. I repeat we can only control our conscious mind. The rest of it we need to learn to manage it. So, when someone talks about mind management, they are referring to the emotional brain and the subconscious mind.

"If you correct your mind, the rest of the life will fall into place." ~ Lao Tzu

How to manage your emotional or chimp brain? Think of your emotional brain as a child. What does a child want?

- wants to feel loved.
- wants to be recognised.
- wants to avoid pain.
- want to feel safe.

Now here's the interesting part. From the lemon experiment we did earlier, we know that our brain does not understand the difference between reality and our thinking. So regardless

CHAPTER 7

of reality, if we think no one loves us, that's what the brain believes and starts acting accordingly. Similar to this, if regardless of the reality, we think we are loved, that's what the brain believes. As we do not have much control over the output (the chemicals it releases and its impact on our system), we must take complete control of the input (the words we speak to ourselves and the images we create in our head).

CHAPTER 8
Human Consciousness

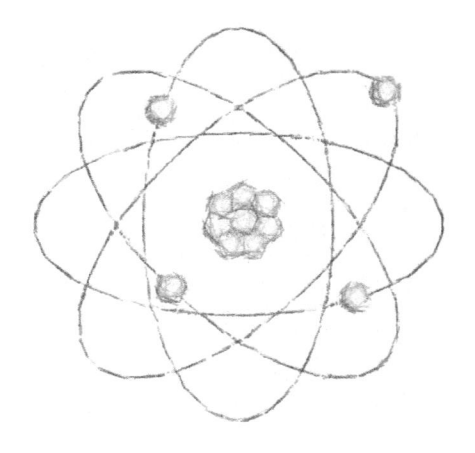

"Somewhere in the innermost recesses of our consciousness lie the answers to the questions all mankind seeks."

~ Syd Banks

Albert Einstein once said, "No problem can be solved from the same level of consciousness that created it," which implies that we must raise our consciousness to erase our problems. But what is consciousness, and how to raise it? As per the dictionary, Consciousness means 'the state of being aware and responsive to one's surroundings'. The key phrase here is the state of being aware. You cannot raise your consciousness unless you are aware.

CHAPTER 8

In the scientific world, there are two conflicting views on consciousness: materialism and dualism. Materialists shun the argument of anything apart from what is physical. They argue that consciousness has evolved through the physical brain. However, no one has been able to explain how this happens. Dualists, on the other hand, believe that consciousness is something outside the physical brain. Both these views fail to provide a satisfactory explanation.

In my opinion, Panpsychism gets closest to explaining what consciousness is and how it originated. According to this theory, consciousness is not a result of our evolution for survival, nor does it come from the brain. Instead, it is something that is inherent in all matter. This means that everything, from trees to rocks to atoms, has consciousness. We live in a conscious universe.

For the scope of this chapter, we will focus on human consciousness. And a simple way to understand your consciousness is to think of it as your awareness. Nothing would ever exist if there was no awareness or consciousness. We make sense of the world around us based on the level of our consciousness. Nothing in the world has meaning apart from the meaning we give it.

4 Levels of Human Consciousness

To further understand consciousness, imagine you are inside a glass elevator. You will have a very limited view when you are at level 0. But as you go higher in the elevator, you can see further. Your view expands. You see a bigger picture and so have a better understanding of what's happening around you. I believe that there are four levels of consciousness. Most of us can operate in two or sometimes even three levels in different situations. Let's discuss this in more detail.

CHAPTER 8

GOD ALIKE
Everything is Me

SUPERHUMAN
Things happen through me

SEEKER
Things happen for me

VICTIM
Things happen to me

Level 1 – Victim Mode

People at this level believe that everything is happening to them. If you find yourself starting a sentence with - only if, but, or because of this, there are high chances that you are operating at the victim level. "Only if I had more time", "but I am too old or too young", "because of my partner, I cannot focus", etc. At this level, we are always busy pointing out what should change. Outside activities, events, or people determine our actions. **We never act; we react**.

Level 2 – Seeker Mode

CHAPTER 8

At this level, you start looking for answers. You believe that things happen for you. When you operate at this level, you become curious instead of passing judgment. You begin to understand the laws of the universe. You believe that everything that happens in your life is for you to learn and grow. You take responsibility for your action. Other people, situations, or events do not influence your actions. You act, not react. Instead of focusing on what should change in situations and others, you ask a better question – What can I learn from this?

Level 3 – Superhuman

I like to call this superhuman level. At this level, you believe everything happening in your life is through you. You are in charge of all that is happening. Most brilliant minds on the planet operate at this level. This is when your inner state becomes unfuckwithable. No person, event, or situation can disturb your inner peace. You become limitless, compassionate, grateful, and a creative genius. You take responsibility for not just your actions but also your inactions. In this state, you are always present and in the flow. Your whole focus is not on what's happening but on what you can do about it. Your consciousness becomes so powerful that you start bending reality.

Level 4 – God-like

The last level is what I refer to as God-like. At this level, you become one with the Universe or Superpower. You believe that everything is you. Some of us may have experienced this state for a short while. Such short experiences are what we call Satori moments. However, it requires constant practice and often years of meditation to attain this state truly. Yogis referred to this state as Samadhi. Sufis called it Turiya. And some prefer the word Enlightenment.

Exercise

Take some time to reflect and journal on the following questions.

- What level of consciousness do you mostly spend your day in? Most people are at different levels at different times.

....
....
....
....
....

- What would it take for you to always operate at Level 2 or above?

....
....
....
....
....

CHAPTER 9
9 Laws of the Human Mind

Humans are the only species on this planet who can use their minds to study their minds, yet most of us waste this huge potential. It usually requires years of practice and research for one to be able to understand their mind. But the good news is that I have done the hard work for you. In this chapter, I am going to share with you the 9 most important laws through which the mind operates. Read these carefully and make notes if needed as I will refer to these in later chapters.

Law 1: *Your mind comprehends information in images.* If I asked you to stop thinking of the white polar bear. The first thing you will do is think of a white polar bear. Because the rest of the words in that sentence do not create a straightforward image.

LAW 2: Your mind is designed to keep you safe and not to make you successful. This means if left on its own, it will always choose comfort over discomfort, pleasure over pain, and easy over hard.

LAW 3: Emotions will always overpower logic. Your emotional or child/chimp brain is more powerful than your conscious/logical mind. Therefore, you cannot control your chimp brain. You must train and manage it. I will share ways in which you can do this in later chapters.

LAW 4: Your mind will always prove your self-image right. Even when it's a false image. So, if you believe, think, and say that you are good at procrastinating, you will be good at procrastinating.

LAW 5: Your brain does not know the difference between reality and your thinking. So, if you are recycling the same thoughts over and over again, you are reliving the same experience psychologically over and over again.

LAW 6: Whatever you focus on, you will find more of. If you focus on problems, you will find more problems. If you focus on opportunities, you will find more opportunities. If you focus on things to be grateful for, you will find more things to be grateful for.

LAW 7: Whatever your mind believes tends to become the reality. Some understand this as the 'Secret', other's call it Placebo. I refer to it as our Mind's ability to bend reality.

LAW 8: We don't experience reality; we experience our thoughts about the reality. Try it yourself. Take any incident from your life. Then think about the positives from it and the negatives from it. You would notice that positive thoughts bring a positive experience of the incident and negative thoughts bring a negative experience of exactly the same incident.

LAW 9: *90% of your response comes from subconscious programming.* But the more active your conscious mind is, the more present you are, the less responsive your subconscious will be. Unfortunately, most of us live the same life on repeat and often also on autopilot. To change past programming and automatic behaviour, you would have to train yourself to be conscious most of the time.

Exercise.

Which of the 9 laws is your favourite? How are you going to use it to improve your life?

....
....
....
....
....
....
....
....
....
....

CHAPTER 10
7 Daily Practices to become the CEO of your brain

Your brain is a very powerful tool. And you know that with great powers comes great responsibility. So, it is your responsibility to control your brain and look after its health. When I talk about the brain, I mainly refer to our chimp brain. As we grow up, many things mess up our brains. Society, parents, peers, and media knowingly or unknowingly cause much damage to our confidence, our emotional management, and how we respond to situations. Our logical mind only starts developing around the age of 7. So, before that, we form beliefs and subconscious programming that may not be based on logical reasoning. The problem is that 95% of our response to situations comes from the subconscious mind. So even when we know that it is not logical to think and respond in a certain way, it gets really hard to manage these responses as they become automatic behaviour. It is not our fault that we are messed up, but if we stay messed up, it is our fault. These practices will help you heal and control your brain.

Practice 1 (Healing): Care Less

Our biggest problem is that we have too many problems. If you care about everything, you care about nothing. There was a point in the history of our civilization when all we cared about was food. As long as we got our two meals for the day, we couldn't care less about anything else. The problem with today's information-overloaded world is that we care too much or, as Mark Manson said in his best-selling book (The Subtle art of not giving a F**k), "We give too many 'F**ks'" Everything we care about takes a part of our energy. We only have 24 hours in a day and a certain amount of energy, so why waste your care on things that don't matter to you? There may even be things that matter to you but are not worth caring for. Let's look at some examples. A cashier at the supermarket is rude to you? Is it worth waiting for the manager to complain about him or her? Who cares? You slept in today and missed your gym? Is it worth ruining the rest of your day by carrying this guilt? You can go to the gym tomorrow or in the evening. Who cares? Not caring is not about being irresponsible but quite the opposite. It is about being responsible and having the ability to respond to more critical tasks at hand.

So, identify the top 5 things that you really care about. These could be your health, happiness, family, business, work, etc. And if the 'problem' does not significantly impact one of these top 5 things, then your first response should be that 'I don't care'.

Practice 2 (Healing): Be Grateful

90% of the things in our life are the way we want them, yet we focus on the 10% that is not the way we want. There is a reason for that. We know that our brain is not designed to make us successful, it's designed to keep us safe. So, in order to be safe, it will always look for problems. This means that if the brain is left on its own it will only have survival thinking. While this was helpful for survival when we used to live in jungles and could not trust anything or anyone, it is harmful to our mental health and our growth. Because whatever you are looking for, you will find more of. So, if you are looking for problems, you will find more problems. If you are looking for reasons to be grateful, you will find more reasons to be grateful.

If there is one question which undoubtedly the whole human species on the planet will answer 'YES' to is 'Do you want to be happy?'. What if there was a connection between this common desire of the human race and gratitude? Some may believe that if you are happy then you will be grateful, and it seems the obvious connection. But what if I ask you to think carefully if this is true? Is it really that happy people are grateful? We all know someone who has everything one could ask for to be happy and they still are miserable. They are constantly seeking something. At times they are not even sure what they are seeking. Then there are also people who have all the misfortune one can have but still radiate happiness. Why? It's because they are grateful for whatever they have. It is not happiness which makes you grateful, but gratefulness which will make you happy.

CHAPTER 10

Gratitude has become the most talked about in personal growth in recent years. In the last decade, several studies have supported the effectiveness of practising daily gratitude. Studies show that people who practice gratitude as a daily ritual are generally more positive, happier and healthier. Research has shown that Practicing gratitude can lower the levels of cortisol, a stress-causing hormone and can boost performance and productivity. Some studies also indicate that people who practice gratefulness, generally sleep better and express more compassion and kindness.

Gratitude helps you shift your vision. By the law of attraction, we attract what we focus on. If we constantly focus on things which we are grateful for, what are we more likely to attract? – More things to be grateful for.

But how to practice gratitude? There are two things which you need to experience Gratitude. Something valuable must be given to you. And the value of this something must be far greater than the efforts (if any) you had to put in order to receive it. What is the one thing which we all are given at any time without making much effort to earn it. It is the present moment. Every present moment is an opportunity which is given to us. We can do anything with that moment and if we did not use it the way we intended, we are given another moment and then another. Start your gratitude practice by being grateful for the present moment. This will also shift your perspective as you will start looking at every present moment as an opportunity.

As a species, our brains have been wired to help us survive. Therefore, we automatically and constantly notice what is broken, undone or lacking in our lives. How can we rewire our brain to experience all these amazing benefits of Gratitude? Gandhi once said, "I cried because I had no shoes, then I met a man who had no feet". Gratitude is about counting your blessings. We do not need to look for reasons to be grateful. If you are reading this, chances are you have too many reasons already. "If you wake up healthy, you are already living someone's dream".

Here are a few techniques you can use to make gratitude a part of your day-to-day life:

1. *Start a Gratitude journal.* Every day note down 5-10 things you are grateful for in your life. It could be as simple as having a roof above your head to maybe some recent achievement or event. Sometimes you can even use the power of gratitude to manifest things you don't yet have. You can say something like I am grateful that more and more money is coming to me, or I am grateful that my dream job will be mine soon. This will put you in the right energy frequency to receive these things. Make this activity a part of your morning or bedtime ritual.
2. *Make a Gratitude board* or collage and stick it on your wall, put it on Pinterest or make it your desktop cover. Whenever you see it, you will be reminded of your commitment to living gratefully.
3. *Accept the challenge of finding the hidden blessing* in every setback. Example: Stuck in traffic? Use the time to meditate (with your eyes open, of course – just focus on your breathing) or listen to an audiobook, then take this as a learning experience of how to deal with an annoyed boss, or how to manage your time effectively to leave work early the next day. Now you can be thankful for this opportunity.
4. *Take conscious control of your life perspective.* Whenever you experience a difficult situation,

remember this quote from Gandhi: *"I cried because I had no shoes, then I met a man who had no feet"*. Then close your eyes and think of 4-5 things you are grateful for. This will boost the neurotransmitter serotonin and activate the brain stem to produce dopamine. You will instantly start feeling better and be in a better state of mind to deal with the situation.

As you practice gratitude, you will notice an inner shift. You will become a happier and more positive person. And as a result, your relationships, productivity, and sleep will all significantly improve over time.

Practice 3 (Healing): Love Yourself

Do you remember the time when you first started walking (maybe you don't – but you get the zest), everyone around was so encouraging, some even clapped and even when you fell, you heard phrases like, "brave boy/girl," "well done," "try again" etc. And you tried, again, and again till you got it. Even little things like holding a spoon and drawing a straight line were celebrated. Fast forward a few decades later, you run companies, manage families, and try every day, but who is celebrating for all you do? Who is encouraging? Do you ever hear words like 'try again,' 'brave boy/girl,' etc.? Half of the time, no one but only you know how hard you are trying or what you have been through. Self-compassion, therefore, becomes your duty to yourself. Appreciate what you have done and what you are doing. Ignore the small mistakes you make along the way, as we are all just learning 'to live.'

You may have learned in people management courses how to avoid negative feedback for staff motivation. How about we stop giving negative feedback to ourselves for our motivation? Self-compassion brings an immediate feeling of peace and happiness. Think about it this way, if you had a friend who you could not get rid of, but the person is constantly nagging and trying to find problems in you. What effect will this person have on you? Now think about what you are doing to yourself when you are self-criticizing. According to Marisa Peer (one of UK's famous mental health coach), 'the most effective way to boost your self-esteem is self-praise'. Marisa has coached many successful millionaires and billionaires, and one of the healing exercises Marisa asks her mentees to do is to write a simple note on their mirror, which reads – 'I AM ENOUGH.' This simple note has brought drastic changes to the life of many individuals, which just shows the power of self-compassion.

Below are a few ways you can practice self-compassion:

- **Pay Attention to your self-talk:** Notice how you talk to yourself, particularly at stressful times or after making a mistake. Instead of saying, 'I am so stupid,' chose to say, 'I made a mistake, but it's OK, and I am learning.'

- **Appreciate and praise yourself often:** I know that we live in a society where modesty is considered admirable. However, no one else is listening when you are talking to yourself. So, next time you do something nice, I give you the freedom to praise yourself, clap for yourself, and celebrate your smallest achievements.

- **Practice Gratitude:** Every morning and just before going to bed, list at least five good things <u>about you</u> and be grateful for them.

Remember, everyone you know will play a long or short role in your life, but the person you see in the mirror will live it all with you. So be nice.

CHAPTER 10

Practice 4 (Healing): Forgive

"Holding on to anger is like grasping a hot coal with the intent of throwing it at someone else: you are the one who gets burned." - Buddha

The quicker you FORGIVE, the happier you will LIVE. In his book Forgive for Good: A Proven Prescription for Health and Happiness, Fred Luskin writes that forgiveness is "taking back your power," "about your healing," and is "for you and not the offender."

So, what exactly is forgiveness? Forgiveness sets you free. It could be defined as giving up my right to hurt you for hurting me. It means I do not have to hear you say, 'I am sorry', for me to move forward with my life. The purpose of forgiveness is to set the victim free. It has nothing to do with the offender.

Anne Lamott defines it the best in her quote - "Not forgiving is like drinking rat poison and then waiting for the rat to die." When we do not forgive someone, it is we who suffer as we are tied to the chains of the negative experience, which always reminds us about it. Isabelle Holland explains this further - "As long as you don't forgive, who and whatever it is will occupy a rent-free space in your mind."

But why Forgive? Forgiving could be extremely difficult, and some may even feel that forgiving someone may not be the fair or right thing to do. After all, the person who has given us pain must suffer and realise they were wrong. Although the real truth is that when we don't forgive someone, we punish ourselves and not the person we are not forgiving. That person may not even realise and care about whether or not we forgive them. Every grudge we hold in our brain acts as fog and damages our mental health and wellbeing. The pain we are causing to our brain by holding this grudge is often multiple times more than the pain that this person inflicted.

When we don't forgive someone, we are continually using a part of our energy to fight this person in our subconscious mind. Imagine if you do not forgive a person for ten years, how much energy you are wasting. Now times this by 2, 3 or more depending on how many people you are not forgiving. All this wasted energy could be used for your growth. When you forgive someone, you are setting yourself free from them and them from you. You are not acknowledging that what they did to you was OK. But what you are doing is saying that you are free from them, and they are from you, as there is nothing you need from them. You can heal you by yourself and do not need their apology or suffering.

Scientists have noted that forgiving can significantly spike the alpha waves in both hemispheres of the brain. Alpha waves are responsible for our intuition, creativity, and learning new skills. The question, therefore, is not why to forgive but why we don't forgive.

We have already discussed that it's not easy to forgive. Many argue that it can be the most challenging thing to do. Although the truth is, it is not difficult at all. As a child, we all were excellent forgivers. Have you ever noticed a child holding a grudge against someone? A child can get annoyed by you, and the very next moment can be hugging and kissing you. This comes naturally to them. We find forgiving difficult because our personalities take over our conscious (or real) selves as we grow up. Our characters are developed by our families, societies, and education.

As we grow, we are taught what is wrong and what is right. We hear stories and watch movies about how the evil or the wronged is always punished in the end. We, therefore, build an expectation that the person who has done wrong to us must realize their mistake and feel sorry. However, in reality, things don't work this way. In the real world, while you are busy thinking that someone must feel sorry for what they did, the other person may be thinking you must feel sorry for what you did. So, you both end up punishing yourself for what you did not do. You did not forgive. If there is one thing you can teach your child, teach them that 'it is more important to be happy than to prove yourself right or the other person wrong.' You are only responsible for your happiness. You are not responsible for teaching others a lesson.

How to Forgive? Before we get to the process of forgiveness, let's make it clear What forgiveness is and is not:

WHAT FORGIVENESS IS NOT

- Forgiveness is not – an act of giving to the offender.
- Forgiveness does not – require one person to apologize or feel sorry.
- Forgiveness does not – pardon the person of their wrongdoings.
- Forgiveness does not – mean admitting what was done or what happened was OK.

WHAT FORGIVENESS IS

- Forgiveness is – a healing gift that you give to yourselves.
- Forgiveness is – freeing up yourself from your past.
- Forgiveness is – claiming back your happiness and realizing that you cannot let one single event or incident from the past dictate your life.

> Forgiveness is – getting rid of the poison from our system.

Let's explain this last point with an example. Suppose a snake bites you. What do you do next? You have two choices. One option is to run around finding that snake and beat it till it feels sorry. But what happens while you are doing this is that the poison spreads inside you. The other option is to forget about the snake and get rid of the poison. Forgiveness is taking care of yourself. Do it for yourself.

Four Steps for Forgiveness:

1. *Increase the blood circulation in Your Brain.* Do a short breathing exercise or meditation to get the blood supply to the prefrontal cortex, a part of the brain responsible for logical thinking, empathy, and forgiveness.

2. *Reframe the experience.* Realize that whatever has happened is nothing about you and everything about the person who did it. It could be because they have grown up in a certain way. They have suffered previously, which has changed their personality. There could be many reasons for people to behave in a certain way. There are two quotes that I find helpful. One is 'Hurt people hurt people,' and the other is 'NO child is born evil.' Remember, we are not justifying that what they did was right. We are only making assumptions to help our brain in the process of forgiveness.

3. *Take responsibility for your feelings.* What happened to you has nothing to do with you and is all about the person who did it. But how you feel, as a result, is your responsibility. Responsibility is the ability to respond. Whatever they did to you is depended on their level of thinking and mindset. However, your happiness is your responsibility. Do not let your feelings be dictated by other people's actions.

4. *Recreate your story.* Recreate your own Hero story. Where you have an Unshakable resilience to deal with the most challenging situations life can throw at you. Think about these people or incidents as a nudge by the Universe to hint to you that it's time to grow. I like the quote from the movie 'My Giant' – 'Without Goliath, David is just a punk kid throwing rocks.' Whatever wrong has happened in your life is what illuminates the greatness of the Hero you are.

Make Forgiveness a daily ritual. Forgive everything and everyone before you go to bed each night. You will feel much lighter and live much happier.

Practice 5 (Control): Win Small Battles

In her book the 5-second rule, Mel Robbins explains that as soon as an event occurs, there is usually a 5-second delay in response from the brain. So, when you want to build a new habit or want to do something, set an alarm for it. And as soon as the alarm rings, start moving within the first 5 seconds. Take some action within the first 5 seconds. This 5-second window is crucial as if you enter into an argument with your (chimp) brain before you take an action, the likelihood is that your brain will convince you to remain comfortable. Focus also on winning other small battles by building daily habits, such as making your bed as soon as you wake up, or a cold shower.

Practice 6 (Control): Pause

Imagine you are working on a computer and have 100 windows open. What would that do to the performance of your computer? It slows it down, right? The same is true for our brains. Every thought is like opening another window. It affects your brain's performance, takes up brain space, and clutters your mind. So, develop a habit of pausing every 60-90 min. Sit wherever you are, close your eyes and visualize closing every thought window. As you close the windows, new thoughts will appear, and it's okay. It's not about the result; it's about the process. So don't get affected by the new thoughts. As soon as a new window (thought) appears, visualise a cross in the top right corner of the window and close it. Take a few deep breaths. Imagine you are filling your body with energy every time you breathe in. And let go of all worry, stress, fear, and neediness to get anything done, every time you breathe out.

Practice 7 (Control): Motivate Your Brain

Your mind (human) is driven by inspiration, but your brain (chimp) needs motivation. There is a thing about motivation. It's like a ripple in the water. When you throw a stone into a pond of still water, you will instantly see the formation of numerous ripples. But what happens if you did not throw another stone? The water will become still. Motivation works in a very similar way. Therefore, to keep our brains motivated, we must continually make an effort. There are two steps you can take to keep your brain motivated:

1. *Have Positive Conversations.* When having a conversation with your brain or what we call self-chatter, treat it as if you were talking to a close friend. It is evident that if we are not kind to a friend, we will lose that friend sooner or later. The same is the case with our brains; if we are not kind when talking to our brain, soon our brain could start separating itself from us/our mind. This is what leads to depression or, in extreme cases, dissociative identity disorder.

   Imagine if you had a close friend who is continually finding fault in you, and you could not get rid of that friend. Well, if you are criticizing yourself, this is precisely the situation you are putting your brain into.

2. *Feed the right information.* The brain works like a computer. It processes the information it receives and produces emotions and reactions. While it's hard to control our emotions and reactions, we can filter or choose the information sent to our brains. One good way of doing so is by taking time out every morning to feed positive information to our brain consciously. This could be done by reading a good book or by using affirmations.

How to use affirmations (a more effective way)?

So, I have been there and done that. 5 AM in the morning, I am sitting with my morning journal and Bulletproof coffee, ready to reprogram my Mind. I write my first affirmation: I am a world-class Public Speaker – my subconscious goes, 'but you are not'. I am Super Rich and Successful – My subconscious whispers – 'Have you looked at your credit card bills?' I am free of anger and full of love – my subconscious cries, 'stop lying to yourself'.

This is what I used to do every single day. Yes, I felt better at that time for some self-praise but inside, it felt meaningless, and nothing changed till I started doing it differently.

The whole purpose of affirmation is to:

1. Shift your identity: So instead of doing something to become something, you first become something, and then the doing part becomes more natural. Let me explain this with an example: Let's say I want to 'become' an Artist. Becoming an artist may seem something out of reach or less possible. What if I decided to shift my identity? I chose to believe I am the

world's best artist. I am the world's best artist is a declaration and not a judgement. Once I start identifying myself as the world's best artist, acting like one will become much easier.

2. Motivate Your Brain: Constant self-criticism and negative feedback from others can be very damaging to our mental health. Affirmations can be a great way to take some time out to acknowledge your efforts and motivate your brain. So, in our example, I can affirm something like, "I am an artist who is getting better at his art every day." Or I am Rich and Successful (Maybe not rich and successful as compared to Jeff Bezos but Rich and Successful when compared to 1-50% of the population on the planet – gratitude), and more money and success is coming my way.

I suggest you write down 5 such affirmations every day.

Remember, it's the feeling which is essential. Just like the lemon experiment, you should feel the affirmation more than you are writing or thinking of it.

CHAPTER 11
Problem Vs Situation
Not every Problem is a Problem

We discussed in the previous chapter how our biggest problem is that we have too many problems. And that we should care less. Make a list of the top 5 things that are important to you, and anything that does not have an impact on these 5 things is not a problem and can be ignored. Remember you can do anything, just not everything. In this chapter, I will share with you a simple tool that you can use to (dis)solve all your problems in 30 seconds or less. This tool has been life-changing for me and my clients. Are you ready? Let's begin.

How to solve a problem in 30 seconds or less?

The first question you ask is, "is this really a problem?" Chances are when you become very present with this question you will realise that it's not something worthy of your time and energy. So, if the answer to the question is no, the problem is (dis)solved.

But if the answer is yes, the next question you want to ask is, "is it one of the top five problems in my life just now?" If the answer is no, then it can go in something that I call the TTKMB list, which is the Things To Keep Me Busy list. Stop labelling it as a problem. You only start working on this list when you have too much time to kill. Problem (dis)solved.

But if you answered yes to the question, which means that it is one of the top five problems in your life just now, then you ask another question, "Is there something I can do about it?" If the answer to this is No, then it's not a problem; it's a situation. Problem (dis) solved. You cannot solve a situation, so stop labelling it as a problem. How to deal with a situation? You work your way around it. For example, if you are out and it starts raining, you don't try to figure out, how to make the rain stop. You open your umbrella and carry on. Or even when you don't have an umbrella, you still carry on, realising that rain is not in your control. Just like some things (situations) in your life will not be in your control.

But if you answered Yes to the question, and there is something you can do about the problem, then it's not a problem. Write down the action steps, allocate some time in your calendar to take these action steps, and then stop labelling this as a problem. Call it a challenge instead. Problem (dis)solved. At the end of this chapter, you will find a flowchart diagram of this approach/tool.

Powerless Vs Powerful Approach

There are two ways to approach a problem: a *powerless approach* and a *powerful approach*. Have you ever been in a situation where you're looking for something, and it's right in front of you, but you can't find it? And then you keep saying to yourself; I can't find it, I can't find it, I can't find it. And so, you can't find it. Next time that happens try changing your inner dialogue to I can't find it. It's right here. I'm going to find it and see what shifts.

Use this same approach to your problems in life and business as well. So, a powerless approach would be – "I can't do this. There is no solution. This is difficult". A powerful approach will be – "This is easy. I got this. There is always a solution".

Dissolving Your Problems Exercise

Take a moment to journal and reflect on one of your problems. Follow the steps in the flowchart on the following page to dissolve this problem and turn it into a situation or a challenge.

....
....
....
....
....
....
....
....
....
....
....
....
....
....

CHAPTER 11

How to (dis)solve a problem in 30 seconds or less?

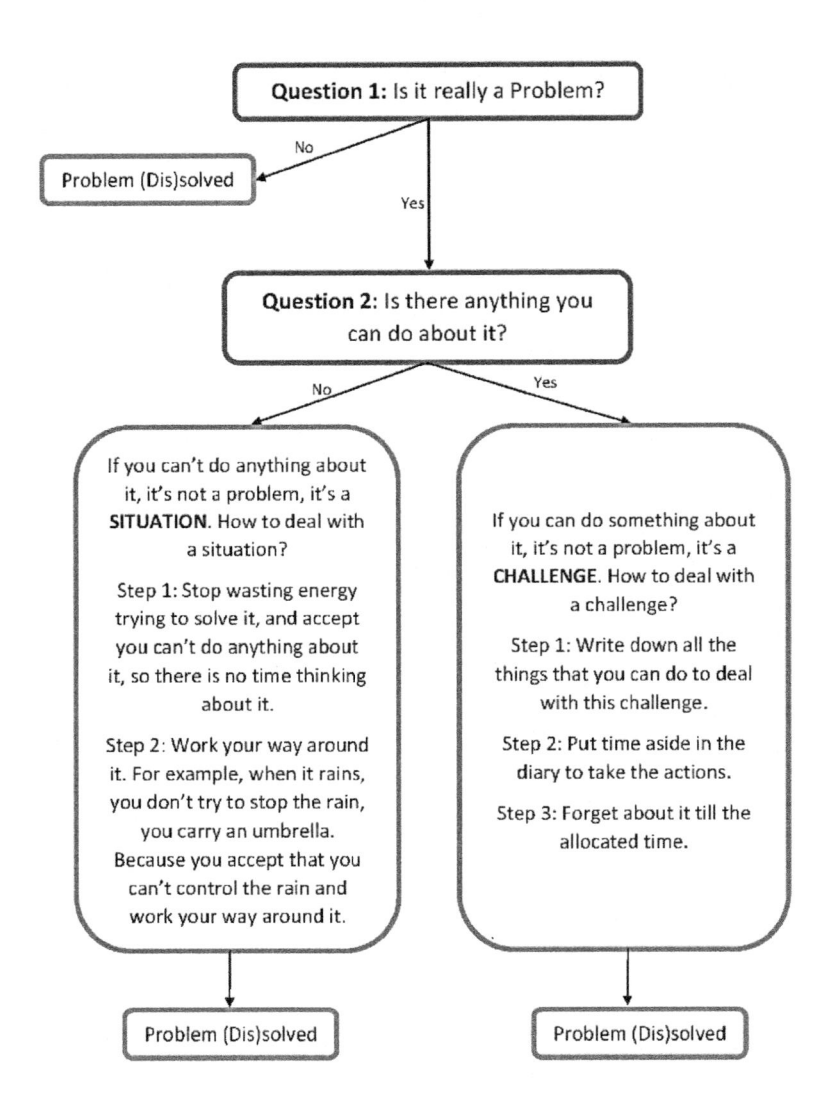

Question 1: Is it really a Problem?

No → Problem (Dis)solved

Yes ↓

Question 2: Is there anything you can do about it?

No:

If you can't do anything about it, it's not a problem, it's a **SITUATION**. How to deal with a situation?

Step 1: Stop wasting energy trying to solve it, and accept you can't do anything about it, so there is no time thinking about it.

Step 2: Work your way around it. For example, when it rains, you don't try to stop the rain, you carry an umbrella. Because you accept that you can't control the rain and work your way around it.

→ Problem (Dis)solved

Yes:

If you can do something about it, it's not a problem, it's a **CHALLENGE**. How to deal with a challenge?

Step 1: Write down all the things that you can do to deal with this challenge.

Step 2: Put time aside in the diary to take the actions.

Step 3: Forget about it till the allocated time.

→ Problem (Dis)solved

CHAPTER 12
Neuroplasticity

The Brain That Continuously Changes Itself

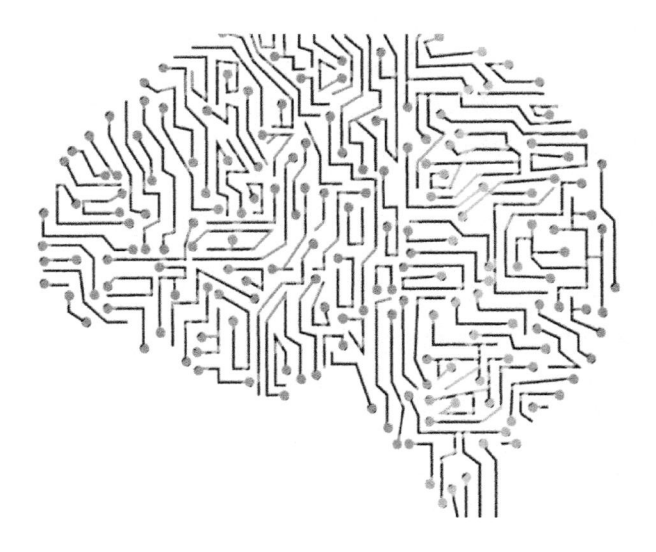

If you have ever heard, read, or thought that our personalities and behaviours shape up as we are children and then they remain fixed for the rest of our lives, then it is time to scrap that belief. The research that supports this notion is outdated. New research in the field of neuroscience indicates that our brain is constantly changing, forming new neural connections and pathways, while losing those that are no longer used. This flexible and adaptable nature of our brain, just like plastic, is referred to by neuroscientists as Neuroplasticity.

How does neuroplasticity work?

Think of your brain as a lively, linked power network. Whenever you think, feel, or engage in an activity, billions of pathways light up. Some of these paths are regularly travelled. These are what we call habits, beliefs, and ways of thinking. Whenever we think in a specific way, carry out a certain task, or feel a particular emotion, we make that path stronger.

But when we choose a different thought or feeling, or engage in a learning activity, we start creating a new neural pathway by making new connections in our brain. Slowly if we repeat this new pattern, the new pathway gets stronger and the old and no longer used pathway gets weaker. This whole process of forming new connections and pathways and losing the old ones is neuroplasticity in action. This means that we can change our behaviours, habits, and personalities at any age. You will find a video explanation of neuroplasticity at https://superhumaninyou.com/book-bonus. I have also included a page below from an excellent article on this topic by NICABM.

CHAPTER 12

NEUROPLASTICITY CAN RESULT FROM:

- Traumatic Events
- Stress
- Social Interaction
- Meditation
- Emotions
- Learning
- Paying Attention
- Diet
- Exercise
- New Experiences

THE **BRIGHT** AND DARK SIDES OF NEUROPLASTICITY

Bright Side:

Neuroplasticity makes your brain resilient.

Neuroplasticity enables you to recover from stroke, injury, and birth abnormalities.

You can learn new ways of being and responding to conflict.

In many cases, you can also overcome depression, addiction, obsessive compulsive patterns, ADHD, and other issues.

Dark Side:

Neuroplasticity means the brain is always learning.

But the brain is neutral – it doesn't know the difference between good and bad.

It learns whatever is repeated – both helpful and unhelpful thoughts, actions, and habits.

Therefore neuroplasticity may entrench depressive, anxious, obsessive, and over-reactive patterns.

nicabm
www.nicabm.com
© 2016 The National Institute for the Clinical Application of Behavioral Medicine

CHAPTER 13
Re-inventing You

"I am not who you think I am; I am not who I think I am; I am who I think you think I am"

~ Charles Horton Cooley

Read the quote from Cooley again and this time allow it to really sink in. We are all born as empty slates. We have tiny bodies and no beliefs, personalities, likes, dislikes, hates etc. Everything we identify ourselves as has been created. We eat food and miraculously change that food into the body and thus create the body (grow bigger). We hear things, we have thoughts, and we turn these thoughts into beliefs. Whatever is created can be ours but is not us. We are the creator and not the creation.

CHAPTER 13

Our thoughts, and so our beliefs, and thus our personalities are influenced by the people around us, media, celebrities, stories, etc. This means that whatever we think we are, is not us; it's just our creation that we created under others' influence. Whatever is created can also be destroyed/uncreated. New research in psychology and neuroscience suggests that our personalities are fluid in nature.

Most of us live our perception of others' perception of us. This is what Cooley is pointing towards in his quote. This is the reason why you behave differently at home than at work, and when with your friends. You would behave the way you think these people perceive you to be. Your brain would help you to maintain your perceived identity. This was a great survival tool when we used to live in the jungle. But it is a hindrance to your growth in today's world.

Imagine what a wasted life it would be if you lived the whole of it, living the created version of yourself that was influenced by someone else. A lot of self-help talk is about being yourself. I say be yourself, but first, know yourself. Because who you think you are, is not you. It's your creation. You are whoever you want to be. Don't think you are stuck with your personality because your personality is just a programmed way of responding/reacting to situations. To reprogram this, you just have to stay conscious and respond differently by consciously choosing different thoughts and actions over a period of time.

Let me explain this by using an analogy. What do you see in the images below?

CHAPTER 13

I am guessing your answer is a fish, a sun, a dinosaur, and a house. But in reality, all you saw was playdough. Your thoughts created a perception based on past information. The problem is if you limit the identity of any of the above as that one thing. It will stay that thing forever. We are like playdoughs. Just because we behave in a certain way, or like certain things, does not mean our behaviour and liking are limited to that thing. This behaviour or like or personality results from others' influence on us. Especially when we were a child. It is time to take control of who you are. You are whoever you want to be in this moment.

But why is it important to take control of who you are or your identity?

There are three ways to change.

1. Information – You learn something new, and you take action.
2. Emotion – You feel something new, and you take action.
3. Identity – You are someone new. And because you are a different person, you act differently.

Your brain will always prove your self-image right

From the laws discussed in chapter 9, we know that our brain will always prove our self-image right. This is another reason why you must start believing that you already are who you want to be. The reason why you don't show up as that person is because of past programming. On a cloudy day, you can not see the sun, but that does not mean the sun is not there. It's always there. Similar to this, who you want to be is inside you; you just have to get rid of the clouds or past patterns and programming. Anytime you don't show up as this person, you are not being you.

We set our own limits by our beliefs

Back in the days, when using animals in the circus was still legal, the circus owners would tie a rope to an elephant's leg when they were still babies. The baby elephant is not strong enough to break the rope and so gives up after trying a few times. As this baby grows up to become a giant elephant weighing 4000 kg, the rope is no more strong enough to hold them. But because they still believe that they can not break the rope, they never do. They spend their entire life tied to it. This is how most of us spend our lives too. We set our own limits by creating a limiting identity.

Reinventing You Exercise

Take some time to sit down and journal who you are. Not who you think you are, but who you truly are. If you could be anyone, what kind of person do you deeply and secretly want to be? That's who you truly are. We will call this the best version of you. Now make a mental image of this best you. And before you make any decision or choice in your daily life, pause for a minute and ask yourself this question – What would the best version of me do?

CHAPTER 13

....
....
....
....
....
....
....

CHAPTER 14
Understanding Emotions

"Your emotions are the slaves to your thoughts, and you are the slave to your emotions."

~ Elizabeth Gilbert

'Emotre', a Latin derivative of the word emotion, means Energy in Motion. You can feel this yourself. Pay attention to how you feel when you are angry or sad. Is our energy/aura expanding or contracting? Notice the same when you feel happy or grateful. Is your energy/aura expanding or contracting?

Emotions are very powerful. After doing something terrible, people often say they did it because they were too emotional or lost control of their emotions. Most of us let emotions run our life, instead of choosing our emotions to run a more fulfilling life. You can hear people saying, 'I have no control over my emotions' or 'I did such and such because I was angry or sad.' But what if there was a model you can use to hack your emotions? What if there was a way to choose your emotions? Which emotions would you choose?

Our emotions are the aftermath of our thoughts. Let's understand this with an example – You are driving to work or a meeting one morning. Suddenly someone dangerously overtakes you. What will be your instinct thought? "What a jerk! Can he not see? Does he not know how to drive? So impatient!". As a result, what will be your emotion? – Anger, Frustration, hatred. But we do not know why that person was in such a rush. What if you knew that the person driving was rushing to the hospital to see their loved one who was counting their last breath? We don't know, right? What if you could think that this was the case? What will be your emotions after this thought? Compassion, Kindness, and Forgiveness. What if we could choose our thoughts based on what emotional state we want to be in? Our emotions affect us more than they affect any other person. In this case, the person who overtook your car is not affected by what you think about him/her; you are.

It is beneficial to reframe situations and use the power of thoughts to feel positive, but it is also important to not judge yourself for feeling in a certain way. When we attach judgment to an emotion, we either try to hide/suppress it, or we fall into the guilt trap. This leads to even more negative emotions. The correct method is to accept the fact that your brain did not like something, and it is communicating it to you by sending energy signals or emotions. Now use your thoughts to reframe the situation. Tell yourself that no matter what happened and who is to blame, I will create action points and note down lessons for things I can do differently. Next, I will reframe the situation to create 'my version of the story,' which supports my mental health and productivity.

Remember that being emotional is not a bad thing. It means your system is working correctly. If you do not feel emotions, it might mean that there is something wrong with your beliefs or the way your brain is operating. This can lead to more significant problems in the long run. The reason why managing emotions is challenging for most is that they start identifying themselves as their emotion.

The key to better Mental Health

The key to better mental health is not manipulating what we think but understanding that 'we think'. There is a lot of effort that goes into positive thinking. But in my experience, positive thinking plus negative thinking leads to overthinking. So, what we must do instead is realise that every thought is not we thinking. And fighting every thought is like trying to calm the waves in an ocean by using more wind in the opposite direction.

Realise the difference between conscious and unconscious thinking. You only need to watch and choose your conscious thinking and stop caring about your unconscious thinking. Any thought that you did not choose intentionally is 'a thought', not your thought. It originates from years of subconscious programming. There's not much you can do about it apart from accepting that it's there, and it's okay.

We live by the philosophy that I think; therefore, I am. Which means we let our thoughts run our lives. When we believe that it's our thought, we do not inquire or question it, and so the emotion that comes from that thought becomes our identity.

CHAPTER 14

We don't say I have an unsupportive thought; as a result, I feel anger. We say I am angry. I am sad.

Instead of believing, I think; therefore, I am, try this, I am, therefore, I think. Which means my thoughts come from me. My thinking is a part of me. My thinking does not define me. So next time you find yourself saying that I am angry, sad, or depressed. Try changing your words to I have angry thoughts or sad thoughts.

We understand this concept for physical pain If you injured your elbow, you would not go around saying that day that you are an elbow pain today. But when it comes to emotional pain, instead of saying I feel sad or I feel angry, we often say I AM sad, I AM depressed, and I AM angry. So our emotions become our identity, and it gets harder to manage them.

Exercise:

What emotions do you identify yourself as? When you think of you, what's the first emotion that comes to your mind? If this is not a positive emotion, realise that it's just a thought and not you. Identify yourself with positive emotion. So whenever you think of yourself, the image you get in your head is embodying this new positive emotion.

....
....
....
....
....
....
....

CHAPTER 15
Present Moment is the only reality

"Realize deeply that the present moment is all you have. Make the NOW the primary focus of your life."

~ Eckhart Tolle

The most commonly asked question in my Mind 2.0 workshops is, 'How does one stay in the NOW?'. This question itself is incorrect. You can only stay in the NOW. I do not know a single person who can stay in the past or future. The problem arises when we 'try' to stay in the now. We make staying in the now, an act of doing. As if we need to do something to be in the now. The truth, however, is that you do not need to do anything to be present or stay in the moment. You just have to realize that there is no other place you can be but in the NOW.

Whenever we are thinking about the past, we are reliving the past in the now. Hence, we are creating multiple copies of the same now in our minds. A now that happened in the past and thought in the present about the same past. If we are thinking about the future, we are considering all that could happen in our lives, mostly negatives. Hence, damaging the now by destroying our state of mind. Nothing can ever be changed in the past, and nothing can ever be created in the future. All the changes and creations happen in the NOW. The only way we can change our Past and affect our Future is by being in the Present.

Past and Future, in real terms, are only thoughts in our heads. Reality and action only happen in the now, the present. Another question which I get asked a lot is, "How can one stop thinking about the past and present?". Let me ask you something, "When do you think about the past and present?" Is it when you are having the best times of your life? When you are living your dream? Or when you are having a tough time? It is often the latter. So one way to turn this around is by looking at the brighter side, focusing on the often ignored good things which are happening in life.

I am not suggesting that you ignore things that cause you pain or unhappiness. All I am suggesting is that you stop ignoring things that are good in your life. 90% of the stuff in our life is usually the way we want them to be, yet we give 100% attention to the 10% of things which are not as per our liking.

Another question which I get asked is that, 'if I stopped thinking about the past and future, how will I learn the lessons from past and plan for my future?' There is nothing wrong with consciously thinking about the past or future when needed. The problem arises when we unconsciously drift into

CHAPTER 15

the past or future and start living life like zombies on autopilot.

We have become accustomed to the modern lifestyle where multitasking is overrated, and thinking about something and doing something else has become a lifestyle. Therefore rewiring our brain to be fully present will require constant practice. You can bring your awareness to the present by just asking certain questions to yourself at several points during the day, such as – What am I thinking? What am I doing? What can I smell? What different noises can I hear at this moment? Remember, if you are not in the NOW, you are on autopilot. You are not living; you are sleeping. It's time to wake up.

CHAPTER 16
The Secret behind "The Secret"

"The day science begins to study non-physical phenomena; it will make more progress in one decade than in all the previous centuries of its existence."

~ Nikola Tesla

In this chapter, I will share with you my understanding of the secret or law of attraction. I don't believe that the secret works the way many perceive it to work. But that does not mean that it doesn't work. I am a science guy, but I also understand that science (at least till now) has its limitations. There is far more of what we don't know as compared to what we know. Even

CHAPTER 16

scientists admit that we don't even understand 1% of the Universe. We don't even know where we are. We know that we are somewhere in the Universe, but where is the Universe? Anyways, that is not the topic of this chapter. The reason why I share this is, that you read this chapter without questioning or believing anything. Read it with an open mind and try the concepts shared to test it in your own life. Don't just discard it, because there is no science to back it up. If you do so, you will miss out on 99% of the universe's miracles.

"The concepts of spirituality are generally just the physics we haven't understood yet."

~ **Nassim Haramein**

I am not a big fan of the word secret, as I don't think there is any secret. I prefer the word 'bending reality. The art of bending Reality is not a new concept. The word was first coined in the biography of Steve Jobs written by Walter Isaacson. In the book, Isaacson explains Jobs' ability to bend reality in his mind and in the mind of others. T Harv Ecker, the author of 'Secrets of Millionaire mind,' said, "What you focus on Expands." According to Ronda Byrne, the creator of the famous movie 'The Secret' – "Your thoughts become things."

Let me explain this by sharing a story with you. There was once a man called David, who was tired of his stressful life. Nothing ever went his way, so he decided to go to this mystical island and find 'inner peace' (whatever that means). When he reached the island, he started looking for a place; he could make his base. The sun was shining high in the sky, and the scorching heat was becoming unbearable. As David kept walking, feelings of doubt began to creep into his mind. He thought to himself, "Is this island really mystical?"; "Did I make a stupid mistake coming here?" His mouth started to become dry, and breathing was getting difficult. He thought to himself, "Wouldn't it be nice if I could get some water?" After a few steps, David saw a stream of fresh water. He quickly put his bag to the side and quenched his thirst and continued to walk. Soon after, he started to feel hungry and thought to himself, "Wouldn't it be nice if I could get some food?" To his surprise, as he walked a few steps, he saw a table with all kinds of delicious food on it. He looked around, but there was no one in sight, so he decided to fulfil his hunger. He thought to himself, "What a COINCIDENCE?"

Once David was done eating, he continued to walk again, but it wasn't too long until he started feeling tired. The sun was still blazing in the sky, so he thought to himself, "Wouldn't it be nice if I could find a tree so that I can rest in its shed?" Suddenly he sees a big banyan tree within a short walk away. The man became delighted and thanked his 'LUCK.' But as he was lying down under the tree, the feelings of DOUBT started to creep again. He reflected everything which had happened in the day and started to feel FEAR in his chest. He thought, "How could all this have happened? What if there is a Devil at this place?" The next moment he saw a big monster approaching him from a short distance. He jumped up and became even more FEARFUL. He thought again, "Oh No! this monster is going to eat me." Do you know what happened next? That's right; he got eaten by the monster. What if I told you that our Universe is very similar to this mystical island and often gives us anything we focus on? However, there are two fundamental rules.

Rule 1: The first rule is that you will not get what you want or ask for instantly; there will always be a time gap. Imagine if you had the privilege to get anything you want as soon as you

CHAPTER 16

want it. You would think of a tiger, and the next moment you see a tiger walking into the room. So, this rule is actually for our good. As often, and especially when overpowered by our emotions, we wish for things that we don't really want. Due to this rule, most of us feel that things never work in our way, or we never get what we want. When the actual reason is, we don't want something long enough for Universe to act on it.

Imagine you are sitting in a Michelin-star restaurant. The waiter comes to take your order, and you place an order of Carrot and Coriander soup with some bread on the side. The waiter takes the order in the kitchen, and the Chef starts working on it. Chef chooses the fresh and best quality carrots and coriander to put in your soup. He cuts them nicely and puts them in some water to boil along with some other spices. It is now 20 minutes since you placed your order, and you are starting to get impatient. Meanwhile, in the Kitchen, the Chef is cooking your soup on a slow flame to get the best flavours. It is now 30 minutes since you have been waiting, and you get annoyed and asked the waiter to change your order.

You say to him that soup is taking too long, and you want to change your order to potato and vegetables instead. The waiter goes into the kitchen, tells the chef, and the chef who was just about to pour your soup into the serving bowl now pours your soup down the drain, and starts preparing potatoes and vegetables for you. With the same process, the chef begins choosing the best ingredients for you and starts cooking your meal. Half an hour goes by, and this time you get even more annoyed and change your order again. The chef who had almost finished making your potatoes and vegetables puts them on the side and starts preparing your new order. Can you see why you are unable to get what you want? Can you see how, because you were not willing to wait for more than half an hour, now you have to wait almost two hours or forever? It is, therefore, imperative to take time to figure out what you want and, once decided, keep your focus on it until you get it. *FOCUS is Following One Cause Until Successful.*

Rule 2: The Universe listens to your emotions and actions more than your words. Suppose you want to be a world-class public speaker, but in your mind, you are continually thinking about everything which could go wrong when you are on stage. What would the universe listen to? The universe will listen that you are afraid to be on stage, and so will make sure you do not get there, or in case if you do get there, it will make sure you do not get there again. Your thoughts and beliefs will dictate your emotions. Therefore, think of constructive thoughts to have supportive emotions. A good practice is always observing your thoughts and swapping them for a more supportive one. You will notice I said supportive, not positive. Cause when you classify your thoughts, or anything for that matter, into positives and negatives, you are using your judgment, and judgment will lead to attachment. We do not want to be attached to our thoughts; we want to be separate from them, to manage them better. Emotions, as we discussed in chapter 13, are Energy in Motion. So, when you align your energy and action towards what you want to achieve, you will become the master creator of your reality (in time, of course). As you master your emotions, the time gap will reduce too.

Think about the Placebo effect. And if you have not heard of the term before or are a bit sceptical about it, you should watch the videos in the book bonuses section of the website at https://superhumaninyou.com/book-bonus. Our body and mind can do incredible things. However, our brain is not so good at identifying what is real or unreal. Remember the lemon experiment we did in chapter 7? Your brain will believe

CHAPTER 16

whatever you tell it. This is a fantastic quality of our powerful brain. It trusts us without asking questions. Use this quality to support your growth, and you will soon start Bending Reality.

CHAPTER 17
How to get Things Done? The Anti-Procrastination Formula

We can get things done using three strategies – Motivation, Commitment and Awareness.

Motivation

One of the most basic strategies to get anything done is to use Motivation, or in other words, you can consciously be in a state where you are motivated. But the problem with motivation is that it's like a ripple in the water. The ripples start when you throw a stone in a pond of still water. But if you did not throw another stone, the ripples would soon stop. Therefore, to get consistent ripples, you need to keep throwing stones. Similarly, if you want to stay motivated, you must consciously motivate yourself every day. There are many ways to do this, such as:

1. Hanging a picture of your favourite quote on your wall.
2. Using affirmations.
3. Reading a book that is aligned with your goals or listening to a podcast, and
4. Working with a coach.

There are two kinds of motivation. Intrinsic – that comes from inside and Extrinsic – that comes from Outside. For intrinsic motivation, you must be clear on why you are doing what you are doing. What's the end goal that you are creating? Keep reminding yourself of this why and you will find that inner motivation. Extrinsic motivation could be achieved by creating external stimuli such as rewards for taking specific actions. These rewards could be as small as a cup of coffee after 2 hours of deep work or a holiday after you finish working on a big project.

But you cannot rely on Motivation as your core strategy, because there will be days when you will not feel motivated no matter what you do. Have you ever been in a situation where you dreaded doing something, but once you went ahead to do it and saw some progress, you start feeling motivated to do more? Motivation is a result and not a prerequisite to taking action. So, a higher level to be in is when You Are Committed.

Commitment

Some people get confused between willpower and commitment. There is a stark difference. You see, willpower is like a muscle; it gets stronger, the more you use it. But commitment is already there inside you; you just have to feel it, access it, and use it when needed.

Here's an example to explain what I mean. Suppose you decide you want to wake up at 5 AM tomorrow morning to go for a run. The alarm rings at 5 AM, and you would probably hit the snooze button, and your excuse would be that you do not have the willpower.

Now imagine you hear your child crying at 5 AM in the morning. Would you need the willpower to wake up and look after her? Probably not, because you are committed to your child's wellbeing. Once you start using this same level of commitment for the things you want to get done, you will never have to rely on willpower or motivation.

Three ways you can stay committed to your goals are:

1. Know your why? Why do you want to do what you want to do?

2. Have no option B? When you do not have option B the only option is to go with option A. Just like, when you hear your child crying, in your mind, there is no other option, than to wake up and look after her.

3. Know your pain and gain. The only reason we do anything in life is to avoid the pain and achieve gain. So, list down all the pains of not taking action and the gains of taking action and then read it as often as possible. But sometimes overcommitment can lead to burnout, exhaustion and overwhelm, especially in times of uncertainty. Therefore, there is also a level above commitment, which is a state when you are awake.

Awareness

CHAPTER 17

In the state of awareness, or when you are fully awake, you take life moment by moment. We all want to create a beautiful and meaningful life, but what we do not realise is that we cannot control life. We cannot control the years that make up that life. We also cannot control the days that make up those years. But there is one thing that we have full control over, and that is what choice we will make at this moment. That is powerful. Because that is all, we need to do, and that is all we can do.

Be awake in every moment and make conscious choices. Not what you want to do. But what you want to create. And what choices are aligned with that? Stop living your life on autopilot. Be awake in every moment, and you would never need motivation or commitment because motivation and commitment are the tools to manipulate your brain. They are useful when your brain controls you. But once you are awake, you become in charge. You control your brain. You may choose to use Motivation or commitment as a bonus strategy, but you don't need them, because you are Awake.

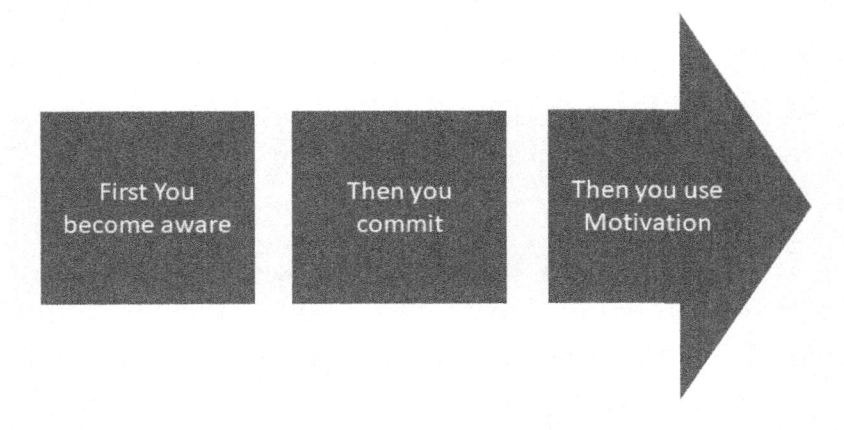

First You become aware → Then you commit → Then you use Motivation

CHAPTER 18
~~Managing~~ Ending Stress

"Stress is the trash of modern-day life. If you do not dispose of it properly, it will pile up and overtake your life."

-Danzae Pace

I believe that whenever we are dealing with a problem, we must first ask three questions: What? Why? And how? In the same order. Let's start by discussing what stress is.

I have spoken to many friends, family, colleagues, and clients. Whenever they tell me what is causing them stress, it is one of these reasons:

CHAPTER 18

1. Money - They do not seem to have enough. Surprisingly, some earn 1,000 pounds a month, while others earn 10,000 a month, but they still have the same problem.
2. Job or Career – They are unhappy with their job or business.
3. Relationships – They are not happy with their relationships in life. This could be with their partners, siblings, parents, or children.
4. Time – This is one thing that gets many people. They never have enough time to do it all.
5. Future – This is the most interesting one. I know many people who have everything but are worried that they will not have it in the future. I call it the What if? Curse. What if the economy is doomed? What if people stop buying my products? What if I lose my job? Etc. You get the point.

What if I told you that all these reasons or any other reason which stresses most people are only due to one thing? You have created an expectation of how things should be, and things are not going as per your expectation. Some people would argue that they need to have expectations for them to achieve their goals. There is a difference between expectations and beliefs. Whatever has happened or is happening is the reality, the truth. It's not going to change. Expecting it to be different is like trying to push the wall. It will not move, but you will waste energy. So instead of expecting something different, try accepting it as it is. When it comes to things in future, start with the belief that things can or will change, but also accept that you cannot control them. You can only choose your actions and your response. A player wins the game not because they expected to win. They win because they played a better game. Focus on your game.

Let's go on time travel to understand what stress does to your body. Imagine a time thousands of years ago when we still use to live in Jungles. You are walking through the woods, and suddenly you see a tiger approaching you. The body triggers a stress response and stops doing whatever it's supposed to do to respond to this life-or-death situation. The brain releases adrenaline and cortisol, aka stress hormones. These are responsible for causing a lot of nuisances in our body, such as insomnia and premature aging. Your heart rate would go up rapidly to move blood through the body. Blood vessels restrict to allow quicker blood movement, which, as a result, will increase blood pressure. Blood sugar and blood lipids increase, so there is more energy to move. Circulation in your gut decreases, because digestion is not a priority when a tiger is chasing you. Immune function drops rapidly as the body needs energy to 'fight or flee.'

The stress response is an essential body function in a life-or-death situation. The problem is that we give too much importance to everyday activities in our life. Therefore, our nervous system cannot distinguish between being chased by a tiger and being stuck in a traffic Jam.

According to research, 90 % of the total doctor visits are related to problems caused by stress. In today's world, most of us are not living our true potential as our body wastes much energy to be ready for an imaginary fight or flee the situation. In the long run, this causes health problems and lower energy levels.

How to End Stress?

Before I answer the question let me be clear that we are talking about ending the feeling of stress. Understand the difference between stress that is caused by the people and situations in

CHAPTER 18

your work and life, and the stress that you feel inside you. We will be talking about ending the stress that you feel. That is the problem. Just like a boat is safe regardless of how deep the water is, as long as the water is outside the boat. Only when the water gets inside it becomes a problem. Similar to this, outside stress is not a problem. Only when it gets inside our mind, we start feeling it, and it becomes a problem. So let me introduce you to two models that, if you adopt in your life, you will never feel stressed again.

Model 1: Good thing, Bad thing, who knows.

I adopted this model from a beautiful old story of a farmer and his son. Allow me to share this story with you:

Once upon a time, there lived a farmer with his son in a tiny village. The father and son did not have many material possessions. They still lived happily and in content. The villagers soon started to envy them and were always curious to find out the reason for their happiness.

One day the farmer decided to use all his savings to buy a horse. Unfortunately, the very next day, the horse managed to escape and run into the hills. The villagers visited to express their sympathy. They remarked, "How unfortunate you are. What happened is bad." To which the farmer said, "Good thing? Bad thing? Who knows?

A few days later, the horse returned and brought with him another six beautiful horses. The villagers revisited the farmer. This time they said, "How fortunate you are. You lost one horse but got back another six." To which the farmer's reply was the same again, "Good thing? Bad thing? Who knows?

CHAPTER 18

After a few days, the farmer's son fell from one of the horses and broke his leg. Even though his leg healed after some time, the injury left him with a permanent limp. The villagers came to visit again and remarked, "How unfortunate. What happened is bad. Who is going to help you in the fields now?" To which the farmer repeated the same words, "Good thing? Bad thing? who knows?"

Soon after that, a war broke out. It was required for all the young men to join the army. However, the farmer's son was spared due to his limp. The villagers once again came to visit him. They said, "You are so fortunate. Your son gets to stay with you, where we are not sure if our sons will ever return home." The farmer's reply was still the same, "Good thing? Bad thing? Who knows?

And this continues. The moral of the story is that Stress is a choice, and if you stop labelling the outcomes in your life as good or bad, then chances are you will start choosing happiness over stress. And you also see opportunities in setbacks that you would have never seen before if you labelled them as a bad thing.

Have you ever observed that a past occurrence that had seemed bad at the time turned out to be a good thing or at least not so bad thing when you look back at it? What has happened has happened and cannot be changed. But how you respond to it is your choice. You can choose to label it bad and increase your suffering, or you can walk away saying, "Good thing? Bad Thing? Who knows?

Model 2: Focus on your actions and not your results

I adapted this model from one of the most beautiful scriptures of all time – the Bhagavad Gita. Imagine a time when we used to live in the wild. A hunter is trying to shoot a deer with his bow and arrow. The hunter is very skilful and has never missed a target before. Does this guarantee that the hunter will be able to get his goal this time? No, not at all. The hunter has command over his arrow and its direction. The hunter can have command of his focus. But the hunter cannot control the deer, who may sense the danger and move at the very last minute. Such is life.

In life, there are things we can control, and then there are things we cannot. Most of the time, things do not happen as planned due to reasons beyond our control. It is, therefore, important not to focus too much on the outcome. Instead, put all your focus on your efforts. Do not celebrate your results; celebrate your actions. It may take some time to adopt these models, but once you do, you will never be stressed again.

CHAPTER 19
Surrender Like a Warrior

"Surrender is like a fish finding the current and going with it."

~ Mark Nepo

If you tell any man/woman of the 21st century that surrender is the only way to salvation, they will look back at you as if you are some loser. After all, our society teaches us to be go-getters, never to give up, and be the warrior who has burnt their boats. But what if I told you that you could be a warrior and fully surrender at the same time? There is only a small difference between a warrior and a raging bull; A warrior has a purpose. Surrendering, in a spiritual sense, does not mean giving up. No, not at all. Instead, it means giving up anything which is not aligned with your purpose. It's not about giving

CHAPTER 19

up control; it's about accepting that we don't have control over a lot of things.

In society today, we have so many management courses that every one of us has become an excellent manager but a miserable human being. To be a good Human being, we just need to focus more on being and less on doing. Practice more surrender and less micromanaging or controlling. We are free spiritual beings and not time-controlled robots. Don't get me wrong; it is essential to have goals aligned with your life's purpose. I believe that every one of us must try to live to our full potential. Have all those beautiful things we want to experience and help as many people as possible. However, micromanagement kills brilliance in us.

Do all you have to do, but with surrender. Bhagavad Gita explains Surrender as one's detachment from the results of their action. Detachment from your results does not mean that you stop taking action. Instead, detachment lets you focus wholly on your efforts without worrying about the results. If you constantly have one eye on the goal, you will have only one eye left to find your way. Detachment from the outcome gives you the freedom to fail and learn, as winning and losing are no more your worry. Now let's look at this argument from a logical viewpoint. What happens when you get detached from the results of your actions – You win over your fear of losing. Fear is the single biggest reason why 98% of us live an ordinary life with an extraordinary soul.

Have you ever found yourself in a mental state where no matter how hard you work or how much you do, you feel that you should do more? A situation where you feel like you must be on constant guard, or something will go wrong? Or the fear that something terrible might happen? Well, whatever you fear will appear. Surrendering is the only way to end all worries. It is putting an end to that restlessness, which may be keeping you up at night. It's not the end of taking action but the end of worrying about the results of your actions or inactions.

When we free ourselves of our fears, accessing the brain's alpha waves becomes easier. Research suggests that alpha waves are more prominent when our brain is calm and in a resting state. Surrendering means the end of resistance. Therefore, surrendering helps increase alpha wave activity in our brains. Alpha waves can dramatically boost our creativity and problem-solving skills. Creativity requires taking a path that has never been taken; it requires freedom and ignoring the norms. This is another reason why surrendering might supercharge your creative genius. Surrendering means giving up control and setting your mind free. It nudges you to set free any hate, grudges, or judgment you have stored in your memory, so there is more space in your brain's workshop.

Sometimes we put too much focus on being right that we sacrifice our happiness for the sake of it. Changing the world is not our responsibility; changing us is. In conflicts over things that have nothing to do with your purpose in life, it is best to surrender than to fight. Choose your battles and surrender to those that are not worth fighting. Then use the saved energy to propel you towards what matters.

True surrender is about letting go, and about accessing flow. It is about putting all your focus on your actions and having an unshakable faith and belief that whatever the Universe brings to you as a result of those actions is for your best. In ancient Vedic literature there is a quote, "If you have one eye on the goal, you only have one eye left to find your way." Surrender is not about giving up control, it's about accepting that we don't have control. When we stop wasting energy

CHAPTER 19

trying to control things that we cannot control, we feel more at ease and grounded. Plus, we have more energy left to focus on the only two things that we can control – our thoughts and our actions.

CHAPTER 20
Feeling the Fear is Not Bad, But Living in Fear is

"Every one of us has a mental waste basket and we would all be a lot healthier if we learned to use it." ~ Syd Banks

So many people feel that their problem is fear, or they want to get rid of the fear. I don't think fear is the problem. Let me give you an example. You are afraid of fire, and that prevents you from getting burned. You fear heights, and that prevents you from falling. You see, fear is not a problem in either of these situations. It is a defence mechanism to keep us safe.

CHAPTER 20

We feel that fear is bad because the stories we hear as we grow up suggest that being scared is bad, especially for men. We hear this all the time, such as Men are not scared. We end up believing that being brave means we should not be afraid. That is impossible. When our body senses danger, it sends a signal to the brain that produces an emotion similar to fear. We cannot get rid of this system, and trust me, you do not want to get rid of this system.

Being brave does not mean the absence of fear. Instead, it means the presence of courage. And courage is doing the right thing regardless of how you feel about it. So, when does fear become a problem? Fear is good to push you to take action. It is good to wake you up. But once you are awake, you want the kicking to stop. In other words, it is okay to feel fear, but it is not okay to live in fear.

We are born with only 2 types of fear. Fear of falling down and fear of loud noises. All other fear is learned. We create it by learning from our parents, friends, society, media etc. What we create can be ours but cannot be us. Understanding this separation is the first step In the rest of this chapter, I will discuss some of the most common forms of fear people have and how to overcome them.

Fear of Unknown

Let me ask you this. Can you tell me what will happen in the next hour, next day, next month, or next year? Can you 100% guarantee that it will happen? Unless you are blessed with some mystical powers, and even then, no one can 100% predict the future. Which means that the future is always uncertain. Nothing is known. But uncertainty is not the problem, our love for certainty is. The fact that we expect things to be certain is the problem. And this problem is multiplied if we start worrying about a negative outcome. Uncertainty does not mean something bad is going to happen. It means anything is possible, good or bad.

Often, we don't suffer the uncertainty, we suffer our IMAGINATION of a future pain that we may or may not experience. Until something bad has happened, it is only an imagination. And the bigger the thinking, the bigger the suffering. Here's a way to reframe your thoughts about this fear. Ask yourself, what's the worst that could happen? And then force your mind to think of the positives of that worst outcome. This will dissolve the fear of that situation. Then remind yourself every time you start having a fearful thought that it's just a thought and it's ok to let it go.

Fear Of 'What They would Think?'

Let's start by defining - who are they? 3-5 of the 7 billion people on the planet. And would you ever truly know what they think? No. You can only make assumptions or predictions of what you think they would think. I used to have a fear of public speaking. I was raised in a family where talking loud and talking too much was considered inappropriate. So, the first few times I had to speak in public, even in class at University, I would literally shiver, my hands would sweat, and I could not breathe. My fear was what they would think if I made a mistake. Until one day, I had this epiphany while speaking on a stage that what I think they would think is my thinking, not theirs. Read that again. Even when we think that our problem is what they would think. In reality, our problem is what we think. And the bigger the thinking, the bigger the suffering.

Here are a couple of ways to reframe this fear. Firstly, understand that whatever they think is their problem, not yours. As we discussed in earlier chapters, we see reality not as it is but as who we are. So, what they see is more a reflection of them than the actual reality. Secondly, understand that whatever you do will be appreciated by some and condemned by others. Whatever you do will never be perfect. Parts of it will be good, and parts will be bad. What they think will depend on which part or 40 bits they are looking at. Continue playing your best game and let others think what they want to think. Remind yourself every time you start having a fearful thought that it's just a thought. It's not the reality, as you cannot mind read and so you would never know what they are actually thinking. You can only guess. So, just let that fearful thought go.

Fear of failure

If I asked you to learn to juggle 3 balls in 3 months, can you do it? Most people would say Yes. But what if I put a condition in there? What if I told you that you must learn to juggle 3 balls in 3 months *without ever dropping any ball*? Can you still do it? Nobody can. You see, failure is inevitable on a journey to success.

Your number of failures is more a reflection of how many new things you try to attempt rather than your individual capabilities. Somebody who spends their time sitting on the sofa watching Netflix can never fail to finish a marathon. It's only the people who participate in it, only the ones who try can also fail. Failure is just proof that you are trying.

Did you or your parents count how many times you fell before you started walking? No, because you focused on walking and not on falling. Then why count your failures in other areas of life? Why focus on what if you fail? Focus on what you need to do to succeed. Once you succeed, no one will remember how many times you failed. Before you fail, any fear of failure is an imagination. After you fail, it is a memory. In any situation, it is just your thinking. And the bigger the thinking, the bigger the suffering. Allow that thought to go, every time it appears.

Fear of Loss

The most common fear of all is the Fear of Loss. But can you really lose something that you do not own? We came into this world empty-handed, and we will leave empty-handed. So, in a way, we are renting everything. Nothing is permanent. Everything is created here and lost here. Losing is not the problem. It's certain, either by fate or by death. Our expectation that things should be permanent is the problem.

Whatever you are afraid of losing, can you guarantee that you will never lose it? No. Can you guarantee that one day you will lose it? Yes. Either by fate or by death. To deal with this fear, remind yourself that nothing is permanent. And until you have actually lost something, it is just imagination or thinking. We know that the bigger the thinking, the bigger the suffering. So let that thought go every time it appears.

Fear of Pain/Suffering

In life, pain is inevitable, but suffering is optional ~ Buddha. Let me share a story with you. Buddha once visited a village where an old lady came to see him. She said to Buddha, "I have been told you can perform miracles. Please help me. My son died 2 days ago. Oh, mighty one! Can you please bring him back to life?" Buddha paused for a minute and then said, "Of course, I will help you. But there is something that you need to do first." The lady replied without any delay, "I would do anything to get my son back." Buddha paused again and replied, "Bring me a handful of mustard seeds. But the seeds must come from a house where no one has ever died." The lady went around and asked in all the houses in the village, but needless to say that she could not find a single house where no one had ever died.

The moral of the story is that pain is part of life. But we don't suffer because of pain. We suffer either the imagination or the memory of pain. Something that happened 10 years ago we can suffer today. Something that has not happened, we can still suffer by imagining that it might happen. We don't suffer the problem or the pain. We suffer our thoughts about the problem or the pain. Once we accept that pain is an inseparable part of life, suffering ends, and growth begins.

Anything in the past is not real it's a collection of thoughts or memory. Sometimes we hold on to it because somewhere, we feel that it's a valuable lesson. But how can it be valuable if it's not adding value? I am not suggesting that you don't learn from the past. I am suggesting that you keep the lesson and delete the memory. Whenever something painful happens, our brain processes the incident in three stages. Suffering, learning, and moving on. Some people can spend their entire life in the suffering stage, while others can move from suffering to learning and then moving on within a few seconds. The question you must ask yourself is, how long am I willing to stay in the suffering stage?

Apart from the tools discussed above, here are three tools that you can use to deal with any kind of fear:

1. **Dissect your fear.** Be Curious. Have you ever witnessed a child who is crying, and you give them a keyring and all of a sudden, they stop crying? It's because they get curious. Curiosity is powerful. You cannot be curious and fearful at the same time. You cannot be curious and angry at the same time. So, ask

yourself questions like, what am I afraid of? Or what are some of the things that are going well in my life? Or what part of my body do I feel the fear? The physical symptoms of fear are the same as excitement, as the brain releases the same chemical for both. So apart from my thinking, is the fear really impacting my physical reality if I don't act on it?

2. **Act or Let Go**. Whatever your fear is, ask yourself if there is anything you can do about it. If the answer is No, then there is no need to worry. As if you can't do anything about something, what's the point in worrying? But if you can do something about it, then again, there is no need to worry. All you need to do is write down the things you can do. Allocate some time to do it and then do it.

3. **Rate Your Fear.** Rate your fear on a scale of zero to ten. Zero being the lowest, things that would not bother you, and ten being the highest, things that would be the worst, such as the death of a loved one or your own. What score would you give your current fear? This will hopefully help you realise that we often make the fear big in our head by our thinking.

4. **Awareness.** Bring some awareness to your fear. Notice what part of your body is feeling the fear. Do you feel it in your head, in your heart, or in your gut? Then close your eyes and try imagining that you are watching this fear. Then slowly try to let go of all your judgements about this feeling. It's neither good nor bad. It's just there. Then slowly try to move this feeling away from your body. It's not about succeeding in this exercise. The very practice of doing this will benefit you.

CHAPTER 21
It's Not About Time Management

One of the biggest myths that most people believe in is that the solution to all their problems is better time management.

The Mindset

The concept of time management is flawed. We cannot manage time because whether we use it or not, we lose it every moment. We all are extremely good at allocating time to tasks. That's the easy part. So, it's not about time management; time manages itself and slowly tick-tocks away. It's about **self-management**; that is what you are doing at this moment.

That's the hard part. And it's about being brutal with what is worth your time, energy, and focus. It's not about how much time you are spending on activities; it's what activities you are spending your time on.

The Challenges

There are three main challenges or things to manage to improve your productivity and performance.

CHALLENGE Number 1 - <u>Time Spillage</u>. You would be surprised by how much time we can waste by just mindlessly scrolling between tasks.

How to stop time spillage?

1. Figure out your average hourly rate. That is the average amount of money you can earn per hour. Now, if what you are doing is not worth that much or more, then you need to stop doing it or find someone else to do it so that you can focus on Income Generating Activities or Life Quality Enhancing Activities.
2. One of the best ways to avoid time spillage is to be conscious of what you do every moment. Practice being present. Throughout the day, ask yourself this question. Where am I?
3. List down 5 things that are most important to you in your life and business. Some examples could be your relationship with your family, your health, generating enough money to support your lifestyle etc. Now anytime you do something that does not help improve these 5 things, you need to ask yourself this question: Is it important? What else can I be doing?
4. Practice *Constructive Procrastination* or the art of saying *Not Yet*.

5. Avoid Multitasking or jumping between tasks frequently.

CHALLENGE Number 2 - <u>Mental Diarrhoea</u>. You would be amazed at how much energy is wasted by constant unnecessary thinking. Practice pauses many times throughout the day. Imagine you are working on your computer with 100 windows open. What does that do to the performance of your computer? It slows it down, right? That's what constant thinking does to your brain. Every 60-90 min, take one minute of pause. Close your eyes and visualize closing all your thought bubbles. Focus on your breathing, relax your body, stretch a bit, and then start again.

CHALLENGE Number 3 - <u>Survival Mechanism</u>. Our brain is designed to deal with urgent things first. Because it's designed for survival. Most important things don't have deadlines. For example, there is no deadline to improve your health. No deadline to put systems and processes in your business. No real deadline for business growth activities. So, it's easy for the brain to procrastinate these things. Create your own deadlines for these things and then communicate this to your brain every day. Set regular reminders and times in your diary to take action. Rate yourself weekly for your actions.

Procrastination is not a behaviour problem. It is a communication problem. The reason why you procrastinate is that you are not constantly communicating to your brain why something is important, and you have not set a deadline and communicated this deadline to your brain. To deal with procrastination, remind yourself why you are doing something, set a deadline for taking action, and block time aside for taking that action.

Tools and Strategies

CHAPTER 21

I find three strategies extremely helpful when it comes to time management or improving efficiency.

The FIRST one is Covey's Time Management Matrix:

Stephen Covey, in his book 7 habits of highly effective people, suggests putting first things first by using a time management matrix. I am aware that most of you would know about this. But you don't really know it if you don't use it. Because knowing without doing is as good as not knowing.

Basically, you need to divide your daily activities into four quadrants, as shown in the image below:

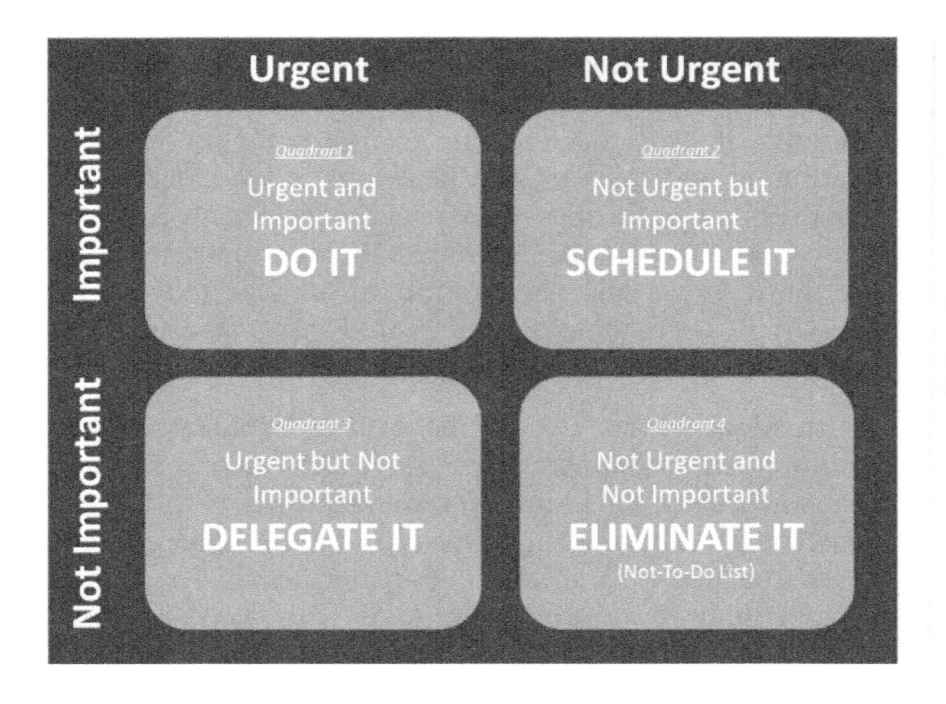

	Urgent	Not Urgent
Important	*Quadrant 1* Urgent and Important **DO IT**	*Quadrant 2* Not Urgent but Important **SCHEDULE IT**
Not Important	*Quadrant 3* Urgent but Not Important **DELEGATE IT**	*Quadrant 4* Not Urgent and Not Important **ELIMINATE IT** (Not-To-Do List)

In the first quadrant are activities that are urgent and important. These activities will be high-priority tasks that must be done today and go on your To-Do list. The second quadrant is activities that are important but not urgent. These are the things that we often procrastinate and put on 'I need to do list' but never actually do, such as starting an exercise routine, creating a business plan, or learning a new skill. If you don't schedule a time for it, it will not be done. In the third quadrant, you put activities that seem urgent but are not important. This is where we waste most of our time. Some examples are replying to emails or texts that may not require an immediate response. Or tasks that do not take our personal and professional life forward. See if you can delegate it, automate it, or eliminate it. If none of these three options seems feasible, then another way to deal with these tasks is also to schedule a time for them, so you are not constantly distracted by them.

The fourth quadrant is not urgent, not important. This is the quadrant where you do activities that waste your time. An example of this could be mindless scrolling through your news feed, watching Netflix or other programs on Television, consuming needless information, or binge-watching YouTube videos. Now an hour of scrolling through your phone and a couple of hours of television every night may seem harmless. But if you multiply those three hours by 365 days, that is.

Some of you may think that you do this for entertainment. But do you really think we need these things for entertainment? Did people not entertain themselves before the discovery of these things? Any entertainment that you do to 'switch off' must be limited to 2-3 hours a week. Instead of switching off, choose entertainments that switch you on. That help to refresh your mind but also enhance your quality of life. For example

CHAPTER 21

– Going for walks in nature, meeting friends and family, meditation, listening to music, playing sports, or taking up a new hobby.

My SECOND Favourite strategy is <u>Deep Work</u>:

In his bestselling book Deep work, Carl Newport talks about the benefits of allocating blocks of time to carry out deep work. This could be extremely beneficial for making progress on important things. Basically, the way it works is that you allocate 60-90 minutes of undistracted time for focusing on an important task. I suggest you start by allocating 90 minutes of your time first thing in the morning for some deep work and allocate this for an important but not necessarily urgent activity, as this is the one that is easily procrastinated. When you get this done first thing in the morning, over the weeks, you will make some huge progress.

My THIRD Favourite strategy is <u>Time Budgeting + Pomodoro</u>

People say time is money. I beg to differ. Time is much more precious than money. If you don't spend money, it will be sitting there. But you cannot choose not to spend time. You can only choose where to spend it. And even if you don't choose where to spend it. You will still lose it, as it's constantly being spent. So any time that is not budgeted will be wasted. Turn your to-do list into time blocks. Not just what you need to do but also when you will do it. Exactly what date and between what hours?

Make sure every hour of every day is budgeted. Budget time not just for your work but also for your personal life. For example, Saturday evening between 5 pm to 7 pm taking wife/husband/partner out for dinner, or Sunday between 11 am to 3 pm, going to the beach with son/daughter, or Monday morning between 6 am to 6:15 am, breathwork and meditation

CHAPTER 21

etc. Below, you will find an image of the planner I use for time budgeting. You can create something similar or buy our journal at https://superhumaninyou.com/books

DAILY PLANNER   / /

High Priority Tasks
- ☐
- ☐
- ☐
- ☐
- ☐

Low Priority Tasks
- ➤
- ➤
- ➤
- ➤
- ➤

Study Goals
- ★
- ★
- ★

Targets

Time Budget	
05:00	
06:00	
07:00	
08:00	
09:00	
10:00	
11:00	
12:00	
13:00	
14:00	
15:00	
16:00	
17:00	
18:00	
19:00	
20:00	

Another important principle to follow, especially if you are working at a Desk, is the Pomodoro Technique. The Pomodoro technique is based on the principle that our brains cannot stay focused without distraction for longer than 45 min. So, after the 90 min of Deep Work in the morning, work undistracted in the blocks of 25 -45 min. Every 25-45 minutes, schedule 5-10 minutes of distraction time, where you use the toilet, check your phone, do 1 min pause meditation (discussed in chapter 10), do a bit of stretching/walking and refill your drinks. You can set the alarm, so you are not constantly checking the time for your next break.

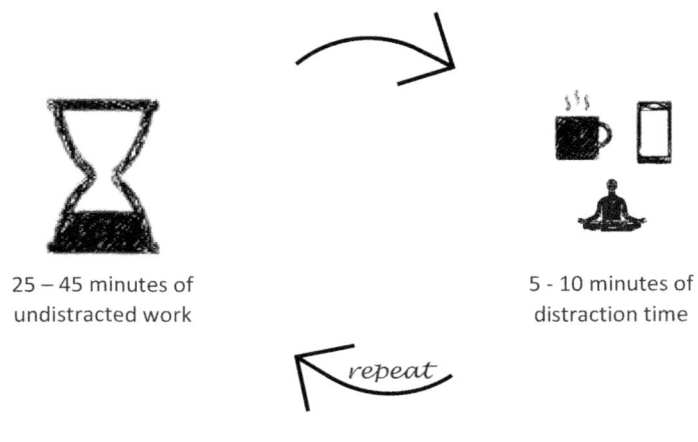

25 – 45 minutes of undistracted work

5 - 10 minutes of distraction time

repeat

POMODORO TECHNIQUE

Skillset

As we have discussed, it's not about time management, it's about self-management. And managing ourselves requires certain skills. The two most important skills to develop for self-management are focus and self-discipline.

Focus: Focus is our ability to concentrate on one task without distraction. It's simple but not at all easy. And the reason it's not easy is that we have trained ourselves for distraction. Over the years, we have practised distraction, and whatever we practice, we get good at. So, in order to improve our focus, we must practice focus. It would be hard because our brain does not like anything that is not normal. But as you slowly practice focusing, you get good at it, and it becomes the new normal.

Two ways to practice focus are deep work and daily meditation.

<u>Self-Discipline</u>: Self-discipline is about being comfortable with being uncomfortable. Do it because it's the right thing to do, not necessarily an easy thing to do. The main ingredient for self-discipline is commitment. Most people believe that they have a motivation problem, but in reality, they have a confusion problem. As Simon Sinek would say: They are not clear on their Why? If your kid is crying at 5 AM in the morning, you would not need the motivation to get up. You would get up regardless of how you feel to look after them. That is commitment. Some ways you can develop the habit of being comfortable with being uncomfortable are - cold showers, making your bed first thing in the morning, not using your phone for the first 2 and following other small healthy rituals that might make you feel uncomfortable.

CHAPTER 22
~~Positive~~ Possibility Thinking

There's a lot of effort that goes into trying to think positive, but in my experience, positive thinking and negative thinking lead to overthinking. So don't consciously force yourself into thinking positive. And don't try to resist negative thoughts. We know that whatever we resist will persist. Just forcing your brain to think positive without any context and without any logic could lead to delusional thinking. Even before anything, realise that things are positive and negative because we label them so. The only reason we are trying to think positive is that we believe that something is negative. To solve the problem upstream we need to tackle that belief.

What if we killed all assumptions and judgements and realised that any situation could have turned out to be worse or better, and could turn into worse or better? I suggest you should practice possibility thinking. You start from a place of looking at things as neutral. Look at them as they are without judging them to be positive or negative. Then realise that no matter how things are, it is POSSIBLE that they could have been worse, and it is POSSIBLE that they could have been better. So, the judgement of positive or negative is just based on what our expectation is and what we are comparing with.

Every situation is a possibility or an opportunity for us to play our best game. In the image on the following page, no matter where our situation is on the graph, it would be possible for it to be more negative and it would be possible for it to be more positive. What we usually do is be **resentful** about why it's not better now and **fearful** about the possibility of it getting worse. What we should do instead is be **grateful** that it's not worse and be **excited** about the possibility of making it better.

For example, let's say you lost some money in business. Now it could have been worse. To lose money, you first need to have it or have access to it. What if you had no money in the first place? Or what if you lost more than just that money? So be grateful that it's not any worse and then be excited about the possibilities. In our example it could be a wake-up call and an opportunity to identify areas of focus in business, so you can take the business to new heights and make even more money. Remember anything is POSSIBLE. You just have to play your best game.

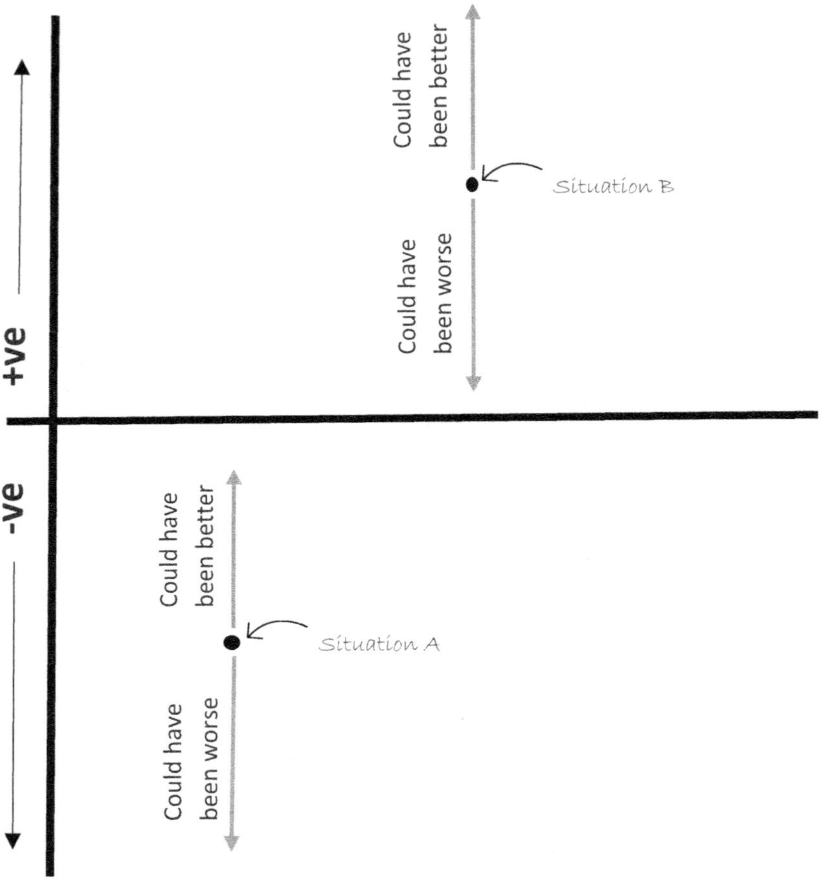
+ve
-ve
Could have been better
Could have been worse
Situation B
Could have been better
Could have been worse
Situation A

REMEMBER RULE NUMBER 6

I want to share an effective technique to deal with your negative thoughts. It's a two-word technique. Are you ready? It's called – DO NOTHING. The nature of the thoughts is that it will come and go. Imagine you are sitting next to a river, and

CHAPTER 22

you are watching the boats go by. As long as you don't jump on a boat, the boat will pass. So don't judge your thoughts as negative and positive. In other words, don't have thoughts about your thoughts. Just let them go and a new thought will appear. And in case if you find yourself in a boat you don't want to be in. Step out and let it go.

Let me tell you a story of two prime ministers. Prime ministers of two separate nations were discussing the trade between the nations. Suddenly the secretary of the resident prime minister came in and started listing out a number of 'urgent' issues. He was so consumed by what was going on that he could hardly speak. The resident prime minister quietly said, "Secretary remember Rule number 6." The secretary immediately calmed down and left after apologising.

After a few minutes another aide of the prime minister came. She was even more distressed as she explained the problems. Prime minister replied quietly again, "Sarah, remember rule number 6." Sarah soon gained her calm, apologised and left. This happened a few times throughout the day. And every time the prime minister quietly repeated the same words, "Remember rule number 6". And the person became calm and left.

The visiting prime minister got curious and just before leaving he asked, "Prime minister! It's astonishing how you managed to calm these people down. If you don't mind, I have a question. What's rule number 6?". And the prime minister said, "Of course! Rule number 6 is – Don't take yourself so seriously". After a minute of silence, the visiting prime minister asked again, "And what are the other rules?". The prime minister replied, "There aren't any".

CHAPTER 22

The moral of the story is that do not take yourself so seriously or do not take your thoughts so seriously. Realise that they are just thoughts, and they have no impact on your life until you give them attention or consider them real. Every thought that you did not consciously choose is a thought, not your thought. Just let that boat go. Remember bigger the thinking bigger the problem.

CHAPTER 23
The Power of Receiving

"Change the way you feel by changing the way you think."

~ **Christine A. Padesky**

We talk a lot about giving but not enough about receiving. Receiving is an art and is equally important. A client once said to me that one of their clients gives them stress. I replied, "Why do you take it?". You can't control what he is giving but you can control what you are receiving. We don't have to take/receive what's been given. And we definitely don't have to carry it with us. We can let go or drop it there and then. So next time a person or situation gives you an experience or emotion you don't want, I am telling you, you don't have to take it. You can drop it there and then. Visualize the experience or emotion as some form of energy (possibly in form of light). Then close your eyes take a deep breath and drop it. Drop it as many times as needed so you do not carry it.

What's outside you is not in your control, but what's inside you, you can control. Wouldn't it be the biggest form of slavery if we let other people control what's happening inside us? We become slaves to their actions. The power of receiving what you choose and not what is given can shift your life trajectory and experience. Let me explain this by telling you the story of two brothers.

The Story of Two Brothers

There were two brothers who lived in a small town. One of the brothers was an alcoholic, and criminal, and use to beat up his family. The other brother was a successful businessman, who was loving towards everyone and was a respected member of society. One day some behavioural psychologists got to know about them. The psychologists were doing research on how the family environment can impact our behaviour and life path.

They decided to interview the brothers. When they went to interview the first brother they asked, "How did you end up choosing this life path?". He replied, "My father was a criminal and alcoholic, and he would come home every day and beat his family. I grew up in that environment, what do you expect me to be?". This made sense to psychologists.

They then went to interview the second brother. They asked, "Your father was an alcoholic and criminal, then how come you become so successful, loving and kind? You grew up in the same environment as your brother." The second brother replied, "Yes, I grew up in a very tough environment. But every time I saw my father coming home drunk and beating us and our mother, I said to myself, I do not want to become like him."

Both brothers were given the same experience, but they experience it differently. And that's because they received it differently. One received it as a curse, the other turned it into a blessing. Because if it wasn't for his father, who knows he would have chosen a normal life, with normal problems. He became successful, loving, and kind because of his father and his ability to choose what he received. I am not saying that their father was right, what I am saying is that the second brother was extraordinary. And if you want to create an extraordinary life, I invite you to be extraordinary too. Don't aim for normal and right. Aim for extraordinary and effective.

How can you choose to receive differently from what is given? It's a three-step process.

STEP 1: <u>Become Aware.</u> To create an inside-out reality, you first have to go inside. So that you can start from that place. To become fully aware, you can do a body scan exercise, while breathing deeply. Take your attention to the top of your head, and then bring it down to your eyes, face, neck, shoulders, hands, arms, fingers, chest, abdominal area, back, thighs, knees, calves, feet, and then toes. The reason why this step is important is that it forces you to become conscious, and so you respond consciously. Instead of reacting based on past programming.

STEP 2: <u>Become Neutral.</u> Let go of any past judgements, assumptions, stories, and expectations. The problem is that we grow up watching and listening to stories, where good always wins. Life does not work like that. It's not about winning every battle, it's about winning the war. And it's not about right or wrong and good or bad, It's about what thoughts and actions are effective and what is ineffective. Right or wrong and good or bad are just perceptions and our judgement of so is based on 40 bits out of the 11 million bits of information. It will never be accurate. Whatever has happened can change my life positively or negatively. If it changes life positively, we can argue that it was a positive thing to happen, or if it changes it negatively, we can say that it was a negative thing. How my life changes are based on my thoughts and actions and not on what happened. We know this to be true from the story of the two brothers. So at this stage what has happened is only a possibility. Good thing or bad thing who knows?

STEP 3: <u>Reframe.</u> What story do I need to believe about what has happened, so it makes a positive impact on my life? That's a life-changing question. Life is just like a game. In this game, your most powerful move is your ability to choose how you will play. You can choose to play the victim, and you may be right that you are a victim of what happened, but where will it take you? On the other hand, you can choose to start with the belief that whatever has happened has happened for some good. I just haven't figured it out yet. Let's keep asking, what good can I create from this?

THE RAINBOW PARADIGM

What's your favourite colour? Let's say it's blue. Now, what if all the colours in the rainbow were blue? Would it look more beautiful? I am guessing the answer is no. The reason why the rainbow looks beautiful is because of its different colours. Our world is the same. People with different opinions, beliefs and personalities are what make the world beautiful and fun.

CHAPTER 23

Otherwise, it will be dull and boring. So, next time when you find a difficult person, someone who does not agree with you, someone who thinks that everything you do is wrong, remind yourself that they are here to make the world beautiful.

CHAPTER 24
How to become Unfuckwithable?

Unfuckwithable

(adj.) When you are truly at **peace** and in touch with yourself, and nothing anyone says or does bothers you, and no **negativity** or drama can **touch you**.
— urbandictionary.com

In a world full of uncertainty, media's fear-mongering, and social media's fake updates, you may think it is impossible to stay sane, let alone be unfuckwithable. But what if I argued that? Nothing outside you can give you peace and nothing outside you can take away your peace. I love the quote from the Kungfu panda movie, "Anything is possible when you have Inner Peace". And that's exactly what being unfuckwithable means. It means having an unshakeable Inner Peace.

Through years of research and working with clients I have identified a few things that you need to remember if you want to have inner peace like Master Shifu, or Yoda. Practising these will not be easy, but it's easier than suffering and the benefits by far outweigh the effort. In essence, there is not a

CHAPTER 24

lot to do but to see, challenge norms, and accept new possibilities.

1. Two things affect people the most - **What others will think about me? And what others will say about me?** When it comes to what others will think. You would never truly know what they think. You can only make assumptions about what they think. So, stop trying to make assumptions and understand that what people think and say is their choice and that what you do is yours. What they think and say is a reflection of their perception and not the actual reality. So, what they think and say is a useful piece of information but not an accurate appraisal of your work or worth.

2. Have no **judgements and expectations**. As e have covered earlier in the book, you can end all your suffering if you put your happiness above right and wrong. I was speaking to a client and they said that a family member really hurt them a few months ago and because of that they are suffering. I suggested, "No one could hurt you (emotionally) unless you allow them to do so". I then asked them if they would get hurt if they did not expect this family member to behave in a certain way. For example, they felt that the family member did not value their feelings. So, the question is would they get hurt if they did not expect the family member to acknowledge their feelings? The response I got was 'No'. And we sat in silence. Sometimes we want things to be fair and right so badly that we sacrifice our happiness for it. How you feel is not your fault, but it is your responsibility.

3. Remember Rule number 6. Don't take your thoughts seriously. **All emotional suffering is caused by thinking**. Something that has happened in past is not real at this moment. It was real when it happened but now it's

only our thinking. Something that we are worried might happen is not real either, it is only our thinking. End the thinking, end the suffering. I understand that it's not easy for everyone to end their thinking. And whatever you resist will persist. So, use the boat analogy explained in an earlier chapter. Don't focus on thoughts that cause suffering. Realise that they are not real and let them go. Don't give them the importance and keep bringing your attention back to your breath or task at hand.

4. Keep your self-esteem high. You are enough. You do not need to do or be anything to be awesome. You are awesome just the way you are. That's the reason why I created a word for the subheading of this book, 'awesomer'. You won't judge a book by just one paragraph, you won't judge a film by just one dialogue, and you won't judge a player by just seeing their one shot. So don't judge yourself for a few wrong actions, or decisions. The fact that you are reading this book already shows that you are among the 10% of the people on the planet who want to get better. Here's an analogy to understand this. Suppose you start eating grass today, will you become a cow? No. Because you are a human. Same way if you had a bad day, bad week, bad month, bad year, or did something bad. It does not change who you are. (It's only what you did). **Your *identity in your mind is like a Thermostat*.** Whatever temperature you set, your reality will sooner or later catch up. So always remember **You are the BEST**

CHAPTER 25
Leading with EQ
How to Positively Influence Others?

Please pay attention to the subheading of the chapter. There are two words that are important – Positively & Influence. Let's discuss each. Often when we talk about influencing people it can come across as some shady tactic or behaviour for manipulation. However, consider this. You are crossing a bridge and you see someone ready to jump off. You stop your car and approach the person. You start talking to them. You use the power of effective communication and emotional intelligence to influence that person to change their mind. Is this influence bad? No, it is lifesaving and also necessary.

As leaders, we lead people in our teams, families and communities. And sometimes in order to help them, you must influence them. Another point to note is that we are talking about influence and not control. We can never control someone; we can only influence them by using communication and emotional intelligence. All great leaders had the skill to move people with their words. To achieve and create great things, you would require a team that believes in your vision.

This is the reason why I have created a 5-step framework for you to follow if you want to influence, help, and serve people in your team, family and community.

STEP 1: **Build Rapport** -> People forget what you said but remember how you made them feel. So, it's important that you focus equally if not more on building rapport than on communicating what you want. I have studied a lot of books and techniques but have found two to be really effective. But before we begin I want to make it clear that in this chapter we are talking about influencing people whom we know. The techniques shared can also help you influence people you have never met before but that's not the focus of this chapter.

- *Make more deposits than withdrawals.* Stephen covey explains in his bestselling book, the 7 habits of highly effective people, that we all have an Emotional Bank Account. The key is to make more deposits than withdrawals. As a golden rule, you must make at least 3 deposits for every withdrawal. The sequence that I follow is DDWD – Deposit Deposit Withdrawal Deposit. Every time you genuinely praise a person, you are making a

deposit in their emotional bank account. And so are building a rapport with their chimp brain. So then when you make a withdrawal or point out an area for improvement, the chimp will not get defensive as it does not see it as an attack, but as genuine feedback.
- *Matching & Mirroring.* Our brain tends to like people who are like us as it does not see them as threats. We naturally match and mirror each other's behaviours when we are around our good friends. However, matching and mirroring can also be used as effective tools to build rapport during important conversations and with people who are not our close friends. How it works is that you match and mirror the most oblivious elements of a person's behaviour during communication, for example, their physiology (physical movements of their body such as posture, crossing legs, or shaking head) and tonality (tone and speed of their voice and choice of words).

STEP 2: **Communication** -> A good measure of how effective your communication was is not what and how you communicated, but what response did you get. If you got the response you intended, then your communication was good, if not then you still haven't fully understood the other person's map of the world. Seek first to understand then to be understood. Have you been in a situation when you have said something to someone many times, and yet they either forget about it or just don't do it? I know I have been. So, what do we do? We say the same thing again, only with added frustration. Albert Einstein said, "Insanity is doing the same thing over and over again and expecting different results". Why? Because not changing is comfortable, even when it's ineffective.

Here's what we should do instead, try to understand why that person is not doing what they have agreed to do. And by understanding, I don't just mean listening to their words, but listening deeply to what's really causing that. Because sometimes that person themselves doesn't know why they behave in that way. So helping them and you to understand more about their behaviour should be the starting point of their conversation. And before you start exploring make sure their defence system is not active by following the rapport-building techniques discussed earlier in this chapter.

Here are the three most powerful, yet underused communication tools:

- *Silence.* "The quieter you become, the more you hear" – Rumi. In any meaningful communication, silence when used in the right places can be way more powerful than any words. Silence helps the person to digest what you have said. Silence also allows them to share more, which in turn helps you to understand more. Silence can also help you to choose your words before you speak. Get comfortable with silence and use it more in communication. Your communication will become exponentially powerful.
- *Empathy.* Empathy is understanding and respecting, not necessarily agreeing with, the other person's view of the world. It's about seeing their problems through their map to understand their challenges and pain. And most importantly it's also about telling them that you understand their situation. Because what you know but don't say, they don't know. So, use sentences like, I understand how you feel, I can see how difficult it is, I agree that it's challenging, or I feel your pain. Every time you disagree with something, start with a statement of agreement. For example, I agree that it's very difficult, but I also believe that you can do this. Or, I agree that it might be unfair, but is it helpful to continue thinking about it?

- *Questions.* If you don't like the answer, change your question. People don't like to be told what to do. So the goal is to ask the right question that helps them see the solution on their own. Powerful questions not only help you to understand someone but also help them understand themselves at a deeper level. Use questions like - What's causing that? Not how to solve the problem but what's causing the problem? And then what's causing that and then what's causing that? Most people try to solve the symptoms and so they keep coming back. Slow down and ask more questions to dig deeper. Do not tell them what to do. Take them to the solution by guiding them with powerful questions. Aim for insights and not information. Because the latter informs, while the prior transforms.

Bonus tips Always use DDWD in your communication. People don't need judgement, they need encouragement. For example, instead of saying why didn't finish your work on deadline, say something like – You are usually excellent at completing things on time. Then what happened? You see, both questions are ultimately asking for the same thing and are arguably the 'right' question to ask. However, the first will get you an excuse and the second will get you a solution. Don't get hung up on what's right. Focus more on what's effective.

Often people respond better to options, than instruction, as this sends a signal to the brain that they are choosing, and not being told. This technique works great with kids. Instead of saying you need to eat healthily, ask them, "Would you like to eat carrots or broccoli tonight?" Instead of telling your employee that they must improve their customer service, ask them, "Would you like to deliver great or excellent customer service?" And then follow up with – "How you can go from where you are to delivering excellent customer service?"

STEP 3: **Kill the need** -> Detach from the outcome. Kill the need for the person to be influenced or changed. What happens is that if we have this 'need' that the person must change then the person can sense it, and their chimp will be on alert to protect them. It will start acting defensive instead of cooperative. When you kill the need, you also kill your frustration and so are in a better position emotionally to communicate effectively.

STEP 4: **Genuinely see the genius in them** -> Have you ever noticed that you behave differently in front of different people? At work, with friends etc. If you believe that someone thinks that you are a calm person, you will naturally try not to be angry in front of them. Whereas if someone always tells you that you have short temper, then no matter how much you try, you will lose your temper in front of them. It's because our brain loves to meet others' expectations. Not what they say they expect, but what you believe they think of you and so expect of you.

Similarly, people will always prove your expectation of them right. They do not do what you say to them, but what they think you expect of them. This is the primary reason why changing someone is hard. Often what we do is reiterate the evidence to them of why they are a certain way. For example – "You always leave the plates on the table", or, "Why are you always so irresponsible?". By doing so we reaffirm the very identity that we want them to change. We know that the easiest way to change is to change our identity. So, if we really want someone to change, then we must help them change their identity in their head. So, regardless of what the evidence suggests you see them as the person you want them to be and then use every opportunity to remind them of this.

For example, instead of saying you are so irresponsible, try saying, "I am really surprised as you are so responsible, what happened yesterday?" Consciously look for even tiny evidence of responsibility and then remind them that you admire how responsible they are. Quantum Mechanics suggests that the Universe is made up of space consisting of fields of vibration, interlinked, integrated and in continuous communication. In other words, we are all connected at the energy level. So a person can often feel the energy of what you think about them, even when you don't say it. So don't just say things, but force yourself to genuinely see the genius in them, if you really want them to change their identity, and so their behaviour.

STEP 5: **Be present.** Keep a part of your attention within you. This will help you stay emotionally stable in any conversation. It will also help you to listen deeply and powerfully. Listen to understand, not to respond. You are a leader, lead from presence.

CHAPTER 26
How to Make or Break Habits on Demand?

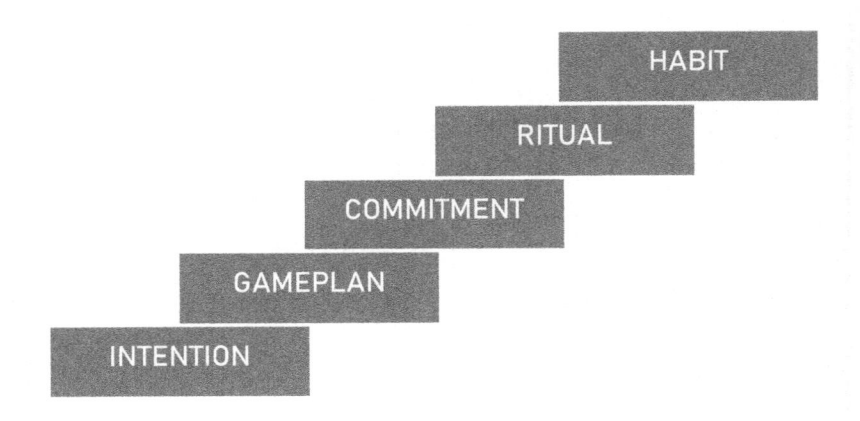

HABIT

RITUAL

COMMITMENT

GAMEPLAN

INTENTION

Before we start, let's discuss what is a habit. According to the dictionary, a habit is a regular practice that is **hard to give up**. Now, this is a really good thing if you have a good habit because it gets ingrained in your lifestyle. But it is not such a good thing if you have a bad habit because if it's hard to give up, what happens is we end up in this cycle where we keep on repeating the same things again and again even when we know that it's damaging our life. I have developed a five-step model that will help you to make or break habits on demand. The 5 steps are - Intention, Gameplan, Commitment, Ritual and the Habit itself.

Let's start with the first one. The first thing to do whenever you want to form a new habit is you must set an **Intention**. And

CHAPTER 26

just thinking about the intention is not enough. You must write it down because when we write down our intention it sends the information to a specific part of the brain which makes it easier to recall. Also, when you write an intention, you engage your mind as well as the body. It tells your subconscious mind that this is something important for you.

The second step is **Gameplan**. You need to write down all the actions you are going to take in order to be able to form that habit. The more detailed the action plan is, the better it is. Some questions that you must consider while creating the game plan are:

- When are you going to start?
- Why are you doing this?
- How are you going to stay motivated? Think about Intrinsic and Extrinsic motivation.
- How are you going to hold yourself accountable? Share that you are going to start or end a habit with as many people as possible. This will help you stay on track as your brain will want to look good in front of these people. You can also create a visual representation of the progress you are making and keep it somewhere you can see it every day.
- Have you blocked time in your calendar if needed?
- What does the end goal look like?
- How will your new habit enhance your life?
- How will your new habit impact others around you and enhance their life?

The third step is **Commitment**. I won't go into much detail on commitment because we have already covered why it's important and how to use it in Chapter 15. Please revisit this section if you need to. What you want to do in this step is commit to following your game plan. But committing once is not enough, because commitment for most people is short-lived. If you do not recommit, your commitment will fade away. You must commit every morning to follow the game plan for that day. Remind yourself every day why it's important to you and that you did not come this far, to only come this far.

The fourth step is Ritual. Research shows that forming a habit is a three steps process. First, there is a cue that triggers the auto-response, and then there's a response to that cue or the action, and the last thing is the reward. For example, if you have a negative habit of smoking usually what happens is people feel stressed, that's the cue, then they smoke (the response), and smoking makes them feel relaxed, which is the reward.

Now if you want to break a habit you must get rid of the cue and the reward. In this example, you want to get rid of the cue which is stress. So, start some mindfulness practices, morning walks, or some other daily practice which will better equip you to deal with the stress and manage that cue. Take care of your health, don't wait till you feel stressed, deal with it beforehand. Then you need to create a similar reward to that of smoking. So, you need to do something else that can help you get the same reward - relaxation. You can take fresh air breaks instead of smoking breaks, where you leave your desk and go for a quick walk.

Another way to deal with the reward is to start disassociating with the perceived reward of the habit. Our brain believes whatever we want it to believe. So, if we think that smoking is going to make us feel better, it will make us feel better. There's a way to flip this around. What you can do instead is try and be present when you're smoking. And associate it with pain instead of a reward or pleasure. Feel how it tastes, and instead of sending the signal to the brain that you're feeling relaxed, feel how it's damaging your body, your lungs, your life, your reputation in front of your kids and loved ones etc.

This way, you'll be able to flip the message around and send the signal to the brain to dissociate smoking from reward and associate it with pain. Our brain learns from repetition, so you will have to do this process a few times as a ritual. You can use the same steps for forming a good habit. Let's say you want to start going to the gym. Set an alarm. Then use this alarm as your cue. Now until a habit is formed you must commit to consciously respond to the cue. Once you have responded to a cue for a number of days (usually around 60), it becomes a habit. So, as soon as the alarm rings, you get ready and leave the house. Don't enter into negotiation or argument with your brain. When there is a cue, you respond, don't think.

As the days go by, you'll form this as a habit and whenever there is an alarm your brain will automatically start thinking about the gym. The next step is the reward. Reward yourself for going to the gym every day. This could be something small like a cup of coffee, or your favourite protein shake. You can also take progress pictures and put them on your desktop, where you can see the reward of going to the gym.

Once you have set an intention, created a clear game plan, committed to that game plan, and finally followed it as a ritual for more than 60 days, you will notice that doing or not doing this thing will become effortless. And that's how you form a lifelong habit.

Exercise

Follow the 5 steps and then use the habit tracker below to track a habit that you want to change for the next 60 days.

Habit Tracker

Fill the little circles for the days when you have performed your ritual.

	M	T	W	T	F	S	S
Wk 1	O	O	O	O	O	O	O
Wk 2	O	O	O	O	O	O	O
Wk 3	O	O	O	O	O	O	O
Wk 4	O	O	O	O	O	O	O
Wk 5	O	O	O	O	O	O	O
Wk 6	O	O	O	O	O	O	O
Wk 7	O	O	O	O	O	O	O
Wk 8	O	O	O	O	O	O	O
Wk 9	O	O	O	O	O	O	O

CHAPTER 27
Why Have a Morning & a Bed-Time Ritual?

"We first make our habits; then our habits make us."

- **John Dryden**

The Chinese Bamboo tree, one of the tallest trees, takes five years to grow its roots. It doesn't break through the ground until 5th year. But when it does come out, it only takes five months for it to grow 90 feet tall—our habits work in a very similar fashion. At first, the change in your performance or productivity may seem insignificant, but slowly the results start compounding. This is also true for bad habits. At first, it may seem that we are still young, or it's not affecting us. But after some time, when the adverse effects start showing up, they compound rapidly.

Difference between Rituals and habits

When you do something about the same time in a similar way and under the same environment every day, the practice is called a ritual. And when you perform a ritual for several days without fail, the ritual becomes a habit. It becomes a part of who you are. In a nutshell, rituals are a compelling way to change your life.

Rituals are not only beneficial for forming good habits; they are also a potent tool to keep us in the right frequency and mindset. Behavioural scientist Michael Norton notes that "in every culture—and throughout history— people who perform rituals report feeling better." When we finish a ritual, it gives the brain a feeling of happiness, satisfaction, and winning. If you incorporate three-morning rituals as part of your morning routine, you have had three wins even before starting the day. Soon you will notice that these smaller wins will transpire into anything big or small you are trying to achieve.

Every time we make a decision, we have to exercise willpower and use our brain. After a number of decisions, our brain loses the capability to make the same quality of decisions. Psychologists refer to this as decision fatigue. This is the primary reason why most successful people have weird rituals. For example, Mark Zuckerberg, just like Steve Jobs, wears the same-coloured t-shirt every day. Ans nearly everyone who is successful in their fields have a morning ritual. So, they don't experience decision fatigue in the early hours of the day. They figure out a routine that works for them and then make it a ritual.

Rituals increase our self-confidence. In a world where everything is uncertain, rituals ensure us that there is a part of our life that is still in our control. The reason why rituals work is that they are driven by commitment and a sense of identity. When you start a ritual, your brain adopts it as part of your identity, and hence you are more likely to stick to it.

Morning Ritual

Morning rituals help you to start the day on the front foot. They help you create your day, instead of surviving it. If you are someone who opens their phone or emails the first thing in the morning, you are training your brain for reaction, instead of creation. I suggest that you start the first hour of the day, sharpening your saw. Robin Sharma calls it the power hour. And if you don't understand what I mean by sharpening your saw, it's a reference from the story of two woodcutters. The first woodcutter started work an hour earlier than the second and stayed three hours later than him yet cut only half the wood as compared to him. What the second woodcutter did differently was to spend an hour every morning sharpening his saw. This allowed him to cut more wood in less time. The irony is that the first believed that he did not have time to sharpen his saw.

Something that I practice for my morning ritual is 6x10. Basically dividing the first 60 minutes of my morning into 6 equal slots of 10 min.

1. I start with 10 minutes of silence. I sit down with a glass of warm water and drink it slowly in silence while taking long deep breaths. Focusing my attention on every sensation in my body such as my breath, the temperature of the water, the temperature of the room etc.

2. The next 10 minutes are spent meditating. If you are not familiar with meditation, I will share a simple technique that you can follow.
3. I then spend 10 minutes stretching or doing yoga. You can do either. The key is to keep your attention inside, keep taking slow deep breaths and stretch to improve blood circulation.
4. The next 10 minutes are spent doing some high-intensity workouts. This could be running, fast walking, a combination of squats and push-ups, or anything else. The goal is to get your heart rate up.
5. The 5th block of 10 minutes is used for journaling. My morning journal includes things I am grateful for, my five-year vision, and some affirmations/ declarations/ reminders of how I create my life. A lot of the things are repeated and that's okay. Because if we can recycle bad things we can also repeat good ones. Our brain learns from repetition. What kind of thoughts do you repeat more? I have included a sample of the format I use. If you want to get our morning journal that includes this and a lot more, you can get it at https://superhumaninyou.com/books
6. Finally, the last 10 minutes are used for a brain dump and time budgeting. In essence, creating a plan for the rest of the day.

Bedtime Ritual

Bedtime rituals are equally important, and my bedtime ritual starts 8 hours before bed. I follow 8321.

8 hours before bed stop drinking/taking caffeine.

3 hours before bed stop working.

2 hours before bed stop eating.

CHAPTER 27

1 hour before bed avoid contact with blue light. So, no screens.

You can also practice something that I call the power down hour. Spend the last hour before bed journaling, meditating, reading a book and preparing things for the following morning. This will not only improve your sleep quality but also help you finish your day on a positive note.

CHAPTER 27

📖 DAILY JOURNAL

🌿 Things I am Grateful For

About me
- _____
- _____
- _____

Material
- _____
- _____
- _____

Non-Material
- _____
- _____
- _____

📋 Five Year Vision

🧠 Affirmations
- _____
- _____
- _____
- _____
- _____

CHAPTER 28
Meditation & Mindfulness

There is enough research to support that Meditation is one of the best things you can do for your mind and brain. Whether your goal is to attain enlightenment or to increase your performance, meditation is a powerful tool to assist with both. Whether you seek the stillness of a monk's mind or to be resilient like a warrior or a bit of both, meditation can help you build an unshakable mindset. Literature has many claimed benefits of meditation, but I will only discuss the scientifically proven ones in this chapter.

One instant and highly studied benefit of meditation is that it helps combat stress. In today's artificial world, where even our food is not 100% natural, our body and mind continuously experience stress and deplete over time. According to research, 90 % of doctor visits are stress related. Meditation can also help you look 10-15 years younger by combating stress and reducing the symptoms of premature ageing.

When our mind experiences stress, Inflammatory chemicals called cytokines, are released in response, which can affect our mood, leading to various mental health problems such as depression. Several studies suggest that meditation may reduce depression by decreasing these inflammatory chemicals.

Meditation reduces stress, which helps your body to relax comfortably; therefore, you will experience better sleep. A good night's sleep is critical for your body and mind to recharge and perform. As an entrepreneur, I have always been about hustle. Due to my busy lifestyle, I found it hard to turn off my mind at bedtime. After I started meditation, I could fall asleep within one minute of lying on the bed (In case you think I am exaggerating, I am not). While before meditation, I would sleep 8-9 hours and still wake up tired. After practising meditation, I only sleep 6-7 hours and feel recharged and full of energy after waking up.

As discussed in earlier chapters, recent research confirms the 'neuroplastic' nature of the human brain, which means that our intelligence is not set at birth – and we can enhance and increase the capacity of our brains in ways once believed impossible. When our body is in 'flight or fight mode,' our brain capacity significantly decreases. Neuroscientists have found that meditation can help Increase our attention span and learning abilities.

You may be aware that our brain is made up of two halves; left and right. The left side is responsible for logic, reasoning, decision-making, and cognitive skills, whereas the right side enables creative thinking and new ideas. Most of us are only good at using one part of our brains, while some top performers can jump between the left and right sides of the brain and use them both effectively as and when required. Researchers have found that meditators have a thicker corpus callosum. Corpus Callosum is a part of our brain which joins the left and right sides and facilitates communication between them.

People who have thicker corpus callosum can use their brains more effectively by using both parts of their brains simultaneously. While they can perform risk analysis and critical thinking to identify a problem using the left side of their brain, they simultaneously come up with creative ideas to solve this problem using the right side. A better connection between two sides of the brain comes with great benefits, such as better focus, super creativity, and enhanced memory.

A SIMPLE WAY TO MEDITATE

The number one reason most people fail to meditate is that they have this idea that you must become thoughtless to be a better meditator. It's like sending a 4-year child for a doctorate at university. It just does not work that way. And you do not have to be thoughtless to get many of the benefits from meditation discussed in this chapter. Just being on the journey is enough to bring significant shifts in your life. To be a better meditator, you have to be an observer of your own life. Have you ever noticed that we find a problem very stressful when dealing with it, but we can give excellent advice if another person is dealing with the same problem, and we are just observing?

So, let's begin the meditation. I want you to close your eyes, take three deep breaths, and observe any thoughts you may have. Don't get carried away with them; just watch your mind and its thoughts. If you get carried away, just say cancel and start being an observer again. If it helps bring your attention back to your breath, every time your mind wanders. Do this for 5-10 minutes in the morning and before bed. Try it for 60 days and you will see such a difference that you will never stop after that. If you want to explore other ways to meditate and would like to take your practice deeper, my book The Power Within helps you with exactly that. You can get the book on amazon or on our website here <https://superhumaninyou.com/books>

Exercise

Use the habit tracker on the next page to track your daily meditations for the next 60 days.

CHAPTER 28

Habit Tracker

Fill the little circles for the days when you have meditated at least once a day.

	M	T	W	T	F	S	S
Wk 1	O	O	O	O	O	O	O
Wk 2	O	O	O	O	O	O	O
Wk 3	O	O	O	O	O	O	O
Wk 4	O	O	O	O	O	O	O
Wk 5	O	O	O	O	O	O	O
Wk 6	O	O	O	O	O	O	O
Wk 7	O	O	O	O	O	O	O
Wk 8	O	O	O	O	O	O	O
Wk 9	O	O	O	O	O	O	O

Now What?

If you have got to this page, without missing any pages in between then it's been an honour to serve you. You are exactly the kind of person I am here to serve. But what now? I hope this book was able to give you a few insights, but **INSIGHTS ≠ RESULTS**. Insight followed by a decision, followed by committed consistent Action equals RESULTS.

So, use the form on the following pages to note down any insights you had, then write a statement of decision next to it and then write the action you are committing to take. My suggestion is to write just three insights. Anything more than three and you risk acting on none. Act on these 3 insights for the next 3 months. Then revisit the book. Read it again. You will notice that you will get fresh insights this time. Note another 3 insights, decisions, and actions. Then spend the next 3 months implementing it. If you can do this with full commitment, I promise you that your life will transform.

I also have a few requests:

- If you liked this book, please leave a review on Amazon or Goodreads. This will help the book to reach more people.
- If this book helped you, gift a copy to someone you know. This could be your team, family members, or friends. It's your opportunity to positively impact someone else's life.
- And if you found this book transformational, do a post on social media about it. This will help you reach and potentially help more people through the contents of the book.

Love who you are but also love who you could be.

Your Biggest Fan

Anurag

INSIGHT	DECISION	ACTION

INSIGHT	DECISION	ACTION

About the Author

Anurag Rai is the founder of Superhuman In You, an organization with a mission to help individuals and organisations thrive not survive and do so without compromising well-being and joy.

Anurag is also an ex-accountant, master NLP practitioner, MSc in Psychological Studies & Organisational Psychology, a certified life and business coach, entrepreneur, and dad to a budding artist. He is now on a mission to help leaders live happier, stress-free, and fulfilled life. This book is an attempt towards that mission.

Anurag provides one-to-one coaching to business leaders and celebrities all across the globe. He offers training and workshops for organisations of all sizes and sectors. He also speaks at events all around the year. For any enquiries, please email anurag.rai@superhumaninyou.com

> **To find out more about Anurag, visit**
> **www.superhumaninyou.com/anurag-rai**

Resources to Help

Blogs: www.superhumaninyou.com/blog

[Enrol Now]
Courses: www.superhumaninyou.com/store

[Read More]
Books: www.superhumaninyou.com/books

[Follow]
Instagram: www.instagram.com/anuragraisuperhuman
Facebook: www.facebook.com/limitless.superhuman
Linkedin: https://www.linkedin.com/in/anuragrai-superhuman

[SUBSCRIBE]
YouTube: www.youtube.com/c/superhumaninyou

Printed in Great Britain
by Amazon